Orestes Brownson and the Problem of Revelation

american
university
studies

Series VII
Theology and Religion

Vol. 223

PETER LANG
New York • Washington, D.C./Baltimore • Bern
Frankfurt am Main • Berlin • Brussels • Vienna • Oxford

Arie J. Griffioen

Orestes Brownson and the Problem of Revelation

The Protestant Years

PETER LANG
New York • Washington, D.C./Baltimore • Bern
Frankfurt am Main • Berlin • Brussels • Vienna • Oxford

Library of Congress Cataloging-in-Publication Data

Griffioen, Arie J.
Orestes Brownson and the problem of revelation:
the Protestant years/ by Arie J. Griffioen.
p. cm. — (American university studies. Series VII,
Theology and religion; v. 223)
Includes bibliographical references.
1. Brownson, Orestes Augustus, 1803–1876—Contributions
in theology of revelation. 2. Revelation—History
of doctrines—19th century. I. Title. II. Series.
B908.B64 G75   231.7'4'092—dc21   2002075709
ISBN 0-8204-5845-7
ISSN 0740-0446

Die Deutsche Bibliothek-CIP-Einheitsaufnahme

Griffioen, Arie J.:
Orestes Brownson and the problem of revelation:
the Protestant years/ Arie J. Griffioen.
-New York; Washington, D.C./Baltimore; Bern;
Frankfurt am Main; Berlin; Brussels; Vienna; Oxford: Lang.
(American university studies. Ser. VII: Theology and religion; Vol. 223)
ISBN 0-8204-5845-7

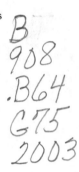

B
908
.B64
G75
2003

The paper in this book meets the guidelines for permanence and durability
of the Committee on Production Guidelines for Book Longevity
of the Council of Library Resources.

© 2003 Peter Lang Publishing, Inc., New York
275 Seventh Avenue, 28th Floor, New York, NY 10001
www.peterlangusa.com

Printed in the United States of America

Dedicated to the memory of my father,

Arie Griffioen, Jr.

(1913–1997)

Bene docet, qui bene distinguit.

Table of Contents

Acknowledgments

I WISH TO thank the staffs of the American Antiquarian Society, Andover-Harvard Theological Library, the Archives of the University of Notre Dame, Marquette University Memorial Library, and the Milwaukee Public Library, Central Branch; the Marquette University Graduate School for granting me the Cyril Smith Family Fellowship, which funded the initial research for this work, and the Calvin College Board of Trustees for granting me the Calvin Research Fellowship, which funded this revision; Robert J. Smith, F.S.C., for his editorial contributions, and Jane E. Griffioen for proofreading the final manuscript.

I also thank the following for permission to reprint from previously published articles.

"Brownson's Early Christology," *American Benedictine Review*, 44, 1 (March, 1993): 58–75.

"Revelation and Reason: Orestes Brownson's Conversion to Catholicism," *Faith and Reason*, XXIII, 2 (Summer, 1997): 141–159.

"Revelation and Progress in the Early Brownson," *Fides et Historia*, XXX, 1 (Winter/Spring, 1998): 15–25.

Preface

IN ORESTES AUGUSTUS BROWNSON'S unpublished papers at the University of Notre Dame Archives is a letter from an unnamed French correspondent who had met Brownson on a visit to the United States in the early 1840s. The correspondent told Brownson that he saw him as a type of the new self-made man that only a free American society could produce. Brownson had not the advantages of nobility, wealth, or a formal education and yet he had brilliant insights into the philosophical, religious, and political movements of modern society. He represented what all human beings could become if they had the freedom to demonstrate their inherent capacities. He arose to a position of prominence in American intellectual circles as editor of one of the more insightful and influential journals in the country, the *Boston Quarterly Review*, on the basis of his own native abilities. He demonstrated clearly the benefits of a free culture for the development of human potential.

Others in Europe, and in the United States, saw the disadvantages of such a culture where freedom led to individualism, pluralism, instability, and a constant change that had no respect for tradition and common values. Here was a culture where individuals' preoccupations with their own internal religious life lead them to ignore the social and political needs of their poorer neighbors. Here was a culture where individuals believed that their successes were the result of their own individual efforts and had nothing to do with the contributions and labors of their own families, their communities, and indeed the culture in which they lived.

Brownson lived in such a culture, and he shared both evaluations of that culture at various time in his life. His own life, in fact, manifested the tensions of these polar opposites. His great struggle was to bring these two dimensions into some kind of intellectual and personally satisfying synthesis.

Arie J. Griffioen tells the story of the internal intellectual struggle and development of Brownson's early years, focusing on a crucial issue in his thought that has to date been overlooked. The issue of revelation, of course, was a central issue for Christians in the eighteenth century as they faced the rise of deism and the challenge of critical reason, and that issue continued to be a central focus in the early nineteenth century. Brownson's religious meanderings put him in contact with a variety of different approaches to revelation, from an almost exclusive emphasis on reason as the bar of revelation, to the supernaturalist rationalist approach of the Unitarians, to a Transcendentalist emphasis upon a primitive and original revelation to the souls of all human beings, to an organic, historical, and developmental approach of the religious socialist Pierre Leroux. Griffioen argues, convincingly, that by 1844 Brownson had reached a synthetic view of revelation, one that wrestled with the variety of American religious approaches and tried to bring them into a grand harmony. Griffioen traces a concatenation of changes and developments in Brownson's thought that helped him arrive at his synthetic vision, demonstrating in the process the variety of American approaches to the issue as American religious thinkers tried to come to grips with the interrelationships of the Bible, reason, religious experience, tradition, and community in understanding what constitutes revelation and its reception.

Griffioen's work is part of a much larger historical effort to re-examine and revise our understanding of Brownson's role in American religious and political life. The twentieth-century re-examination began with Arthur M. Schlesinger, Jr.'s generally sympathetic *Orestes A. Brownson: A Pilgrim's Progress* (1939). Schlesinger raised up Brownson from obscurity and made him a significant player in his *Age of Jackson* (1945). Since that time numerous books and articles, and over forty dissertations, most of them within the last thirty years, have been written on Brownson's life and thought. Nonetheless, he is still not widely known in American academic life. He is rarely read in the areas where he had received a considerable amount of attention and reaction during his own day—in the areas of theology, philosophy, politics, literature, and social reform.

Brownson's thought is worth re-examining not only because he reflected so much of early nineteenth century American intellectual life, but also because many of the issues that he addressed transcend his own times and continue to interest intellectuals. His primary interests were religious and his religious views affected his philosophical, political, literary, and social perspectives. Griffioen presents here a careful study of one of those central religious issues that divided the early nineteenth century and that still separates religious communities today: an understanding of the role of revelation in the Christian life. Even if they do not agree with his synthetic approach, religious thinkers will find this study of Brownson's perspectives on revelation an insightful and serious discussion of the various factors that must be considered in responding to the issue today.

Patrick W. Carey

Introduction

FOR THE PURPOSE of gaining insight into the evolution of nineteenth century American intellectual life, few thinkers can be engaged with greater value than Orestes Augustus Brownson (1803–1876). This is true not only with respect to social, political, and economic developments, but also with respect to the philosophical and theological foundations upon which these former are erected. This study examines the development of these philosophical and theological foundations of Brownson's thought during his public career as a Protestant, prior to his conversion to Roman Catholicism in 1844.

Research into Brownson's Protestant thought has been seriously hampered by the obscurity and unavailability of many of the primary sources and the simple lack of significant secondary sources. Scholars have had to rely almost exclusively upon Henry Brownson's twenty volume collection of his father's work.[1] This collection contains only thirty-four articles from the pre-Catholic period and these only for their supposed Catholic tendencies. Moreover, these articles date from 1836–1844; nothing previous to 1836 is contained in the collection. It is simply inadequate for dealing with Brownson's Protestant period.[2]

As a result of these problems, many scholars are unaware of the earliest developments of Brownson's thought and consequently fail to treat the accessible sources in their proper relation to previous development. Reliance has been placed almost exclusively upon Brownson's autobiographical writings for knowledge of his early career.[3] Though at times helpful, these fascinating and tempting personal accounts are often written decades after the fact and are frequently anachronistic. This study avoids this problem by attempting to pay exclusive attention to the primary sources produced during the periods treated.

Research for this project has identified over two hundred articles, books, and pamphlets from Brownson's Protestant period not included in Henry Brownson's *Works*. Though scholars have examined some of these materials, much has been left untreated. His writings as a Universalist minister from 1826–1829, which reveal the earliest public manifestations of his evolving thought, have been practically ignored.[4] No unified and complete examination of the primary sources of Brownson's Protestant thought has been undertaken.

The few secondary sources that deal with Brownson's Protestant period tend to suffer from reading his Roman Catholic experience back into his Protestant thought. In works that attempt to account for his conversion, only the last few years of his Protestant period are treated and the same anachronistic errors are frequently committed. One of the results of these tendencies is the failure to adequately acknowledge the continuity from Brownson's Protestant career to his Roman Catholic career. For example, Brownson's critique of transcendentalism emerges years before he begins to consider Catholicism seriously. Moreover, those works that attempt to deal with his entire Protestant period are less concerned with his philosophical and theological development than with his socio-political thought. In the final analysis, the secondary sources, though occasionally helpful, are rarely of any crucial significance for this study.[5]

I argue in this study that the development of Brownson's doctrine of revelation constitutes the means by which the philosophical theology that undergirds his thought as a Protestant is most thoroughly disclosed, for its development occurs within the post-Enlightenment attempt to justify Christian belief by establishing the conditions or grounds for the possibility of revelation. As such, Brownson's doctrine of revelation permeates all of his many intellectual pursuits, and does so in spite of his multifarious religious affiliations and experiences.[6]

However, the emergence of the doctrine of revelation within the American context has not been adequately elaborated to date. Though this study attempts no such comprehensive treatment, Brownson's thought provides excellent insight into the antebellum American intellectual context and offers a vantage point from which to view the problem of establishing the conditions for the possibility of revelation within that context. This is especially true when one considers his shift from Enlightenment to Romantic categories and his awareness—often in distinction from his contemporaries—of the philosophical dimensions of the problem of revelation.

The human race, Brownson believes, is advanced through the disclosure of divine revelation. A strong American optimism permeates his writings as he looks to his country to lead the human race into an age of unprecedented enlightenment and prosperity. The progress of the human race is a constant theme in his thought and his evolving doctrine of revelation provides the means of effecting and articulating this fundamental concern.

Brownson's preoccupation with these matters continues throughout his life. However, this study deals only with his often neglected Protestant thought (1826–1844). In addition to providing a manageable period for intellectual engagement, Brownson's career as a Protestant thinker reflects his essential philosophical and theological concerns, as well as the emerging synthesis through which his thought achieves a maturity and integration previously lacking. While an exposition of Brownson's doctrine of revelation during his public career as a Protestant thinker lends itself to increased insight into his thought as America's leading nineteenth century lay Roman Catholic apologist, the choice of 1844 as the termination of this study allows his Protestant thought to stand on its own as an enterprising and perhaps original intellectual response to the pressing religious problems of his day as they arose out of the antebellum American post-Enlightenment milieu.

Within this historical and intellectual context, Brownson develops a synthetic theology of revelation. The development forms an odyssey that begins in an intellectual environment of Lockean empiricism modified by Scottish Common Sense Realism, embraces the impact of Romanticism and the influence of French eclecticism, and ends in a synthesis of thought that propels Brownson into the Roman Catholic Church. This study distinguishes four periods in Brownson's Protestant thought that correspond to these influences and out of which his synthetic theology of revelation emerges.

During Brownson's first period (1826–1832), revelation is discerned and demarcated primarily through empirical evidence, reflecting the employment of Enlightenment categories. The second period (1833–1836) is largely a reaction to the first and is marked by an emerging Romantic intuitionism whereby revelation is appropriated immediately by the knowing subject. The third period (1836–1841) exhibits the impact of Victor Cousin's French eclecticism as Brownson attempts a synthesis of his two previous extremes, and the fourth period (1842–1844) marks the refinement of his synthesis through the adaptation of Pierre Leroux's doctrine of "life by communion." A key to Brownson's synthesis is his recognition of the limits of reason. By means of the doctrine of life by communion, revelation as fact comes to be asserted *a priori*. Reason can only disclose the objective intelligibility of the fact of revelation; it cannot reveal the fact itself.

Consequently, Brownson's major contribution as an American antebellum philosophical theologian consists of his ability, through the doctrine of life by communion, to assert the necessity of revelation as mediated through the object. His insistence upon the necessity of establishing objective grounds for revelation constitutes an important historical response to Immanuel Kant's limitation of the role of "pure reason." Since reason cannot reach the noumenal, the mediation of the object is required.

Moreover, Brownson's emphasis upon the communal implications of revelation remains of value today. His discontent with a mere private revelation communicated immediately from God to the individual stands in vivid contrast to the individualism that characterizes much of American religiosity—in Brownson's time and in our own. Therefore, Brownson's maturing Protestant thought can be entertained by those concerned not only with the doctrine of revelation, but also the communal means by which that revelation is mediated and known.

Historical and Intellectual Context

The tendency of Enlightenment thought to reduce the rationally knowable and defensible to the empirically demonstrable signaled a crisis unprecedented in the history of Christian thought. From the origins of Christianity through the Reformation period of the sixteenth century, divine and supernatural revelation was assumed as an article of faith and the essential means by which nature, history, and experience were interpreted. The rise of modern science in the late sixteenth and seventeenth centuries removed that assumption altogether. By the eighteenth century, the doctrine of revelation appears for the first time as a distinct locus of theological apologetics, designed to counter deism.

It is the legacy of John Locke (1632–1704) that Brownson most frequently invokes during the earliest period of his Protestant career. It is also Locke who is most frequently disparaged during Brownson's reactionary second period. Though an examination of the early intellectual context of Brownson's thought must also take into account the ascendancy of Scottish Common Sense Realism in antebellum America, as well as emerging Romantic influences, a brief review of Locke on the subject of revelation serves to illustrate the eighteenth century background of the problem of revelation in Brownson's thought.

Locke certainly did not ground the entirety of religious belief in rational demonstration. He did not question the fact of a revelation communicated by God, the truths of which were to be acknowledged in addition to those uncovered by the light of reason. Rather, the matter to be addressed concerns the relation of revelation and reason, or more specifically, how we are to judge the authenticity of divine revelations in order to grant them the assent of faith. The judgments concerning the authenticity of divine revelations are intended to counter rationalism on one hand and enthusiasm on the other.

In *An Essay Concerning Human Understanding* (1690), Locke attempts to clarify that which can be reasonably believed about Christianity, that is, the extent to which genuine knowledge concerning religion can be asserted and the manner in which this knowledge is attained. He begins by distinguishing between that which is according to reason, that is, "such propositions whose truth we can discover by examining and tracing those ideas we have from sensation and reflection, and by natural deduction find to be true or probable"; that which is above reason, that is, "such propositions whose truth or probability we cannot by reason derive from those principles"; and that which is contrary to reason, that is, "such propositions as are inconsistent with or irreconcilable to our clear and distinct ideas. Thus the existence of one God is according to reason; the existence of more than one God is contrary to reason; the resurrection of the dead above reason."[7] The problem of revelation concerns especially those propositions that are above reason. The assent to these propositions, which are not made through the deductions of reason, "but upon the credit of the proposer, as coming from God in some extraordinary way of communication," Locke calls *faith*. Likewise, the extraordinary means of communication is termed *revelation*.[8]

Consequently, the question of revelation becomes one of establishing the criteria for accepting "the credit of the proposer," whereby that which is claimed may be reasonably known to have come from God and not another. Three criteria are listed in the *Essay*: One may not assent in faith to propositions deemed to be contrary to "clear intuitive knowledge,"[9] nor to propositions about "new simple ideas," that is, those that allegedly are received through a "sixth sense" and cannot be spoken of intelligibly.[10] Finally, the assent of faith is to be given only to those propositions that are capable of being understood.[11]

The justification for accepting propositions above reason is found especially in the "outward signs" that provide empirical evidence of a divine revelation. Locke's more detailed treatment of these questions in *The Reasonableness of Christianity* (1695) identifies these signs as miracles and fulfilled prophecies.[12] According to this work, Jesus is he who proposes the revealed propositions to which the assent of faith is required. His credibility is established, first of all, on the basis of his identity as Messiah, as the remarkable fulfillment of an extraordinary prediction. In the second place, miracles lend credibility to Jesus' claims by plainly demonstrating the power of God.[13]

The question at issue, however, is whether the outward signs represent mere sensible ideas, that is, whether Locke is simply reducing the problem to the level of the empirical, thus allowing reason to function as the final arbiter of what is to be considered genuine revelation. It is precisely at this point that the Lockean problem of revelation is most evident: "Whatever God hath revealed is certainly true; no doubt can be made of it. This is the proper object of faith, but whether it be a divine revelation or no, reason must judge."[14] Reason is itself termed "natural revelation," the means by which God communicates truth insofar as it is empirically accessible. Consequently, revelation is "natural reason enlarged by a new set of discoveries communicated by God immediately, which reason vouches the truth of, by the testimony and proofs it gives that they come from God."[15] Though the content of revelation is above reason, it is only according to reason that the revelation can be deemed authentic and trustworthy.

Brownson's early thought typifies this "telescopic" notion, whereby revelation is understood to consist of an enlargement of natural reason, and according to which revelation may in no wise contradict natural reason. Brownson does not move away from his earliest position until he begins to recognize the difference between affirming the reality of divine revelation and reducing that affirmation to a proof for its divine authenticity. However, in his second period, Brownson merely shifts the burden of proof from the empirical object to the knowing subject through an affirmation of intuition as the epistemic means of appropriating an immediate revelation delivered by God to the soul.

Indeed, it is the doctrine of intuition that frequently functions as the epistemological means by which late eighteenth and nineteenth century thinkers attempted to distance themselves from empiricism. With respect to the problem of revelation and reason, the doctrine of intuition allows for the immediacy of divine activity within the finite and human, thus counteracting deism.

But the doctrine of intuition certainly is not original with post-Enlightenment figures. I. T. Ramsey, for example, contends that Locke's arguments contain an implicit appeal to intuition as the means by which the propositions are initially known, and should be taken into account before Locke is accused of deism.[16] Brownson would probably concur, for his early doctrine of "intuitive perception" is derived from Locke, though again, Scottish Realism must also be taken into account.

Whether or not Ramsey is correct, he recognizes that much of what follows from Locke in the eighteenth century tends in the direction of deism by virtue of the Enlightenment preoccupation with the natural sciences. The increasing clarity of nature achieved through the power of reason challenged traditional Christianity's assumed exclusive right to interpret nature and history. Though natural theology rises to the defense of the claims of Christianity, its own efforts proceed from the rationalist presuppositions of the day, effectively reducing the claims of Christianity to a search for evidence that would lend revelation some degree of authenticity and Christian belief a reasonable foundation.

By the late eighteenth century, the attempts of natural theology to defend and rejuvenate Christian belief in a divine and supernatural revelation had largely acquiesced to the rigors of modern scientific inquiry and had finally succumbed as it tried unsuccessfully to free itself from such skeptical indictments as those of David Hume. It becomes increasingly evident that if a supernatural revelation is to be allowed, the necessary rational conditions or grounds for its possibility would have to be posited initially. It is this search, at least in part, that signals the emergence of post-Enlightenment thought and the beginnings of a movement toward Romanticism.

To a degree, Immanuel Kant's (1724–1804) critical philosophy may be viewed in this light. On one hand, his critique would seem to complete the Enlightenment challenge to revelation by restricting human knowledge to the phenomenal realm, effectively depriving religion of its rational basis. On the other hand, the delimitation of "pure reason" to the phenomenal allows the delineation of a realm of faith, namely, the noumenal. The delineation of a noumenal or transcendental realm functioned as the intellectual justification for the identification of a seat of human nature through which God and his revelation can be known immediately. Under the influence of Romanticism, this seat of human nature often comes to be identified with a religious sentiment or intuition.

However, as is evident in the thought of the German Idealists and the American Transcendentalists, Kant's delineation recasts the problem of revelation into one of reconciling subject and object is such a way that would allow for an authentication of subjective experience as corresponding to objective reality. The problem of revelation became the problem of establishing the reality and credibility of the object, as corresponding to subjective experience. This re-casting of the problem of revelation is evident in the transition from Brownson's first period to his second, while his growing awareness of the intellectual problem of establishing the credibility of objective reality motivates his attempt to form a harmonious synthesis of subject and object, forming the impetus for his third and fourth periods.

When Brownson begins his public career as a Universalist minister in 1826, these factors were only beginning to come into play. Scottish Common Sense Realism had replaced Lockean empiricism as the predominant school of American philosophical thought and Romantic influences had not yet arrived from Europe. Locke's name was still revered and invoked by many, including Brownson, but empiricism in America had been modified significantly by the Scottish school.

Derived primarily from the thought of Thomas Reid (1710–1776), Scottish Realism emerged in opposition to the alleged skepticism of Hume, who maintained that no logically necessary connection between distinct existences can be intuited or demonstrated. Reid contends that Hume's point of departure entails the impossibility of rationally demonstrating the correlation between subjective ideas and external objective reality, thus inviting skepticism. Reid teaches that the authenticity of external objects is assured in that the conception of them which forms in the mind is always accompanied by an intuitive belief or original judgment in regard to the existence of the object:

> Such original and natural judgments are…a part of that furniture which Nature hath given to the human understanding. They are the inspiration of the Almighty, no less than our notions or simple apprehensions. They serve to direct us in the common affairs of life, where our reasoning faculty would leave us in the dark. They are a part of our constitution; and all the discoveries of our reason are grounded upon them. They make up what is called *the common sense of mankind*: and what is manifestly contrary to any of those first principles, is what we call *absurd*.[17]

Therefore, knowledge is more than mere mental reflection. It is characterized not by an associational conclusion, as Hume would allege, but by an original judgment that presupposes the permanence of both the knower as subject and the knowable as object. Truth is based on the naive consciousness of common sense. In the human mind there are self-evident propositions that stand in no need of reasoning. There is a court of appeal which is not an intellectual abstraction, but consists of practical and theoretical principles. This court of appeal provides the subject with the necessary conditions for knowledge of objective reality, that is, with self-evident natural judgments and suggestions that are experiential, universal, essential to belief, and prior to all argumentation. In essence, the court of appeal consists of intuitive presuppositions guaranteed by God and affirmed by the consensus of humanity.

Brownson's Universalist publications in the 1820s do not manifest the maturity of thought necessary to articulate a nuanced epistemology, but rather a somewhat naive appropriation of the rationalism characteristic of the time. It is difficult to identify his intellectual tradition, for he usually fails to identify his sources. His relative youth and lack of formal education also contribute to the difficulty. But his earliest writings seem to presuppose the Lockean view of the mind as a *tabula rasa*, though by 1829 one detects the allowance of intuitive self-evident principles, betraying the influence of Scottish Realism. For example, it is not at all clear what Brownson means by "intuitive perception" in his 1829 "An Essay on Christianity."[18] Yet, it seems to function as an epistemological transition from his naive assimilation of Enlightenment rationality during his first period to his assertion of a religious sentiment common to humanity in his second; from his "telescopic" view of revelation as closely identified with empirical evidence to an immediate and intuitive revelation closely identified with the knowing subject. Moreover, the notion of the common sense of humanity as embodied in the history and tradition of the race becomes increasingly important for Brownson during the third and fourth periods of his Protestant career.

Brownson's doctrine of revelation during his second period reflects the influence of Romanticism. Without underestimating the influence of William Ellery Channing (1870–1842), whose 1828 sermon "Likeness to God" had a profound impact upon Brownson, the seemingly abrupt turnabout in his thought during his second period is traceable to the effects of Romantic themes and impulses, especially Benjamin Constant's (1767–1830) doctrine of the religious sentiment. A Romantic intuitionism allows Brownson to posit his notion of a religious sentiment as the epistemological means of appropriating an immediate revelation of God to the soul.

In the shift from Enlightenment to Romantic categories, the problem of revelation is altered. In the struggle to retain a place for divine revelatory activity, the Enlightenment problem is articulated primarily in terms of the relation of the natural and the supernatural, the latter of which is posited on the basis of such evidence as miracles. But the Romantic problem becomes one of establishing the credibility of the object. By allowing a revelation immediately intuited by the subject, the necessity of empirical evidence is eliminated. The object loses its previous status and eventually ceases altogether to function as a mediator of the divine.[19]

In America, the clash of these competing minds resulted in the "miracles controversy" fought between the Unitarian rationalist Andrews Norton (1786–1853), and the Transcendentalists, among whose ranks were George Ripley (1802–1880), Ralph Waldo Emerson (1803–1882), and Theodore Parker (1810–1860).[20] Rejecting Romantic intuitionism, Norton argues for the necessity of miracles as confirmation and proof of the divine mission and teachings of Jesus. The Transcendentalists, on the other hand, argue for the divine presence within the human soul as confirmation of the claims of Christianity. Known immediately through intuition, the supernatural does not require such external and objective confirmation. Brownson, siding with the Transcendentalists, de-emphasizes the importance of miracles, claiming they are no proof for the claims of Christianity or the mission of Jesus.[21]

But Brownson, who typically saw the problems of his own positions in the thought of others, recognizes that the question is essentially one of revelation. He senses correctly that to cast intuition in the role of an immediate subjective appropriation of revelation inevitably gives itself over to Idealism, according to which the intuition functions as a "unitary principle" from which all of reality is posited and assessed.

Brownson recognizes this tendency toward Idealism in the thought of the Transcendentalists. Though diverse in their opinions on a variety of matters, the Transcendentalists are united by their belief in the ability of the mind to intuit immediately the realities of the supernatural world. One need only look inward for the evidence of divine revelation. As Brownson drifts away from the Transcendentalist movement toward a synthesis of subject and object, Emerson and Parker frequently act as the foils for his evolving thought.

Even during his second period, when a strong subjectivistic approach is taken, Brownson manifests a concern for the significance of the object and its correspondence to subjective experience, most acutely expressed in relation to God and God's revelation. This concern explains Brownson's preference for the French eclectics, especially Victor Cousin (1792–1867), who sought to reconcile subject and object in a fashion not unlike Scottish Realism, though drawing upon Romantic categories.[22] It is Cousin's thought that allows Brownson to move beyond the Transcendentalists by means of a synthesis that begins to re-establish the status of the object and allows it to function as the mediator of revelation to the subject.

Finally, during his last period as a Protestant, the synthesis is refined through the influence of the doctrine of "life by communion," derived from the French Romantic thinker Pierre Leroux (1797–1871). The doctrine equips Brownson with the intellectual tools necessary to achieve a synthesis that allows the object to function as the mediator of revelation to the subject, without sacrificing their distinction. To his satisfaction, this synthesis functions in such a way as to establish the conditions for the possibility of revelation, thus justifying Christian belief.

Selection of Categories

The chapters of this book correspond to the four periods of Brownson's Protestant career outlined above. After appropriate introductory remarks, each chapter is divided into five sections dealing with the relation of revelation to reason, nature, history, Scripture, and Jesus. The criteria for selection of these categories is threefold. First, they reflect areas of concern to Brownson within which the problem of revelation is articulated and according to which his positions emerge. Quite simply, the categories chosen reflect Brownson's own preoccupations. Second, the categories reflect the historical and intellectual context within which Brownson's thought develops. Frequently, the categories demonstrate the influences of various influential figures, as well as the effects of Romanticism and French eclecticism. Third, the categories must reflect the attempt to form and refine the synthesis of thought that characterizes the third and fourth periods of his Protestant career.

The choice of the category of reason is obvious. While the other four categories constitute the media through which revelation is communicated, the category of reason concerns the means by which revelation is epistemologically appropriated. Indeed, the search for the conditions necessary for the possibility of revelation is fundamentally epistemological, reflecting the rise of the natural sciences during the Enlightenment, Lockean empiricism, Humean skepticism, Kant's critique, the role of Scottish Realism, and the emergence of Romanticism.

The category of nature is the primary medium of revelation during Brownson's first period, reflecting the dominance of Enlightenment categories and the intellectual climate in America prior to the arrival of Romanticism. The subjectivism of his second period shifts the emphasis away from nature, at least in its Enlightenment sense, but it reemerges in the third period as he attempts a synthetic reconciliation of subject and object. Under the influence of Romanticism, his understanding of nature becomes less static and more organic during his third and fourth periods.

History is relatively unimportant to Brownson during his first period. But through the influence of Romanticism, it emerges as a fundamental category of his thought. During his second and third periods, history is granted a positive and progressive status, and during the fourth period it emerges as a crucial element of his synthesis.

The category of Scripture is probably the weakest of the five, according to the criteria listed. It does not play a decisive role in Brownson's attempt at synthesis, though it surely exemplifies it. Nevertheless, it is included by virtue of its importance to the era and the extended treatment Brownson affords it. One simply cannot ignore the role of Scripture within this context.

The role of Jesus in Brownson's Protestant thought evolves from that of a communicator of truths in his first period to a symbolic representation of the ideal embodiment of the religious sentiment in his second. The shift of emphasis from Jesus' teachings to his person continues during his third period until the role becomes incarnational and mediatorial during the fourth. As such, the role of Jesus becomes a key integrating factor in Brownson's synthesis, though never in isolation from the other categories.

One final introductory word is in order. There can be no doubt that the synthesis of thought that Brownson achieves has a great deal to do with his conversion to Roman Catholicism. However, it is not the intent of this study to deal with the conversion itself, or the rationale behind it. While recognizing his movement toward Catholicism, this study will allow Brownson's Protestant thought to stand on its own as an original and enterprising intellectual response to the religious preoccupations and problems of his day.

CHAPTER ONE

Revelation and Empirical Evidence (1826–1832)

THIS CHAPTER ADDRESSES the earliest period of Brownson's public career, spanning his publications as a Universalist minister in upstate New York, his brief flirtation with "free inquiry," and his early Unitarian years. During this time, Brownson's conception of revelation is unnuanced and only beginning to develop. Revelation tends to be closely aligned with the communication of empirical evidence to the *tabula rasa* of the mind, primarily through the medium of nature, though to a lesser extent through the media of history, Scripture, and Jesus.

The Enlightenment reduction of the range of the intelligible to the empirical is clearly operative in Brownson's thought during this period. To be known, the objective truths of revelation must be reduced to the natural and identified with empirical evidence, for Brownson posits no epistemic means whereby a supernatural revelation can be appropriated and, therefore, no conditions allowing for the possibility of a supernatural revelation. Consequently, Brownson's immature thought consists of little more than a natural theology, allowing only a tentative and supplemental revelation that must be everywhere consistent with the dictates of reason. No contradiction between rationality and revelation is allowed.

The tendency to identify revelation with the natural and empirical results in Brownson's struggle to retain some relevance for revealed religion, especially with respect to social, political, and economic progress. Likewise, the acquisition of revelation on the part of the subject is largely an act of rational assent according to varying degrees of evidence supplied by the object to the senses. At this time, however, young Brownson had read little philosophy and simply lacks the maturity and thoroughness that would mark his thought in coming decades. Rather, his is a somewhat uncritical and optimistic use of the prevailing rationality, frequently resulting in sterile pronouncements.

In the final analysis, the tentative and supplemental revelation consists of no more than an "enlargement" of the natural that cannot be known with rational certainty, only believed. In effect, that which cannot be comprehended by the senses is relegated to the inconsequential. In much the same fashion, religion tends to be reduced to morality.[1] Brownson's inability to posit conditions for the possibility of a supernatural revelation reduces the pursuit of individual and social amelioration to the advancement and discoveries of the physical sciences. The cause of individual and social ills lies in human ignorance of the laws of nature.[2] This stark and rather utilitarian approach soon leads Brownson to despair of religion altogether and to affiliate for a brief time with the Workingmens' party of New York, until his religious sensitivities are reawakened by Channing's sermons.

After a brief contextual introduction to the emergence of the Universalist denomination, this chapter consists of sections dealing with the relation of revelation to reason, nature, history, Scripture, and Jesus. As is evident below, the categories of history, Scripture, and Jesus fail to be decisive; however, they play minimal roles, anticipating later developments. Reason and nature are central, the former as the means of epistemic appropriation, the latter as the primary medium. The chapter concludes by addressing Brownson's transitional period of doubt and free inquiry after leaving the Universalists, and his early Unitarian years during which revelation becomes increasingly identified with an inner inspiration.

Universalism

Brownson's ordination to the Universalist ministry on June 18, 1826, signals the beginning of his career as a preacher and a writer.[3] By the time of his affiliation, the Universalist church had undergone considerable change from its earliest form as embodied in the thought of British immigrant John Murray (1741–1815). Raised an Anglican Calvinist, Murray was influenced by the eighteenth century theologies of John Wesley (1703–1791) and James Relly (1722–1778), especially the latter's argument for the actual salvation of all humanity through union with Christ. Arriving in New Jersey in 1770, Murray planted the Rellyan doctrine in soil made fertile for the germination of new sects in the aftermath of the Great Awakening. By 1779 the first Universalist church had been formed in Gloucester, Massachusetts, with Murray as its pastor. By 1825 there were nearly 300 Universalist congregations and 150 ministers.[4]

Murray's American contemporary Charles Chauncy (1705–1787) shared his rejection of the doctrine of eternal damnation. But Chauncy's reluctance to publish his treatise on universal salvation, *The Mystery Hid from Ages and*

Generations (written in the 1750s, but not published until 1784) partly out of fear of being identified with Murray, sheds light on the dynamics of early Universalism. For the most part, Murray remained within traditional Calvinist categories, merely modifying them to achieve his Universalist purposes. Chauncy's Arminianism stood in sharp contrast to Murray's simple extension of the scope of election to all humanity.[5] Furthermore, Chauncy and his colleagues remained the established clergy of New England, while Murray and the early Universalists found their closest allies among such dissenting groups as the Baptists and Quakers—allies also with respect to the belief in an absolute separation of church and state.[6] As a result, Murray was often regarded by his established contemporaries as a rabble-rousing itinerant and fanatic, doing more harm than good for the liberal campaign against traditional Calvinism. The Universalist movement likewise was perceived by the mainstream as sectarian.

For the most part, the Universalists were to remain a reactionary group located on the fringe of turn of the century New England denominationalism. But while their theology and experiential piety would continue to be based in reaction to the perceived harshness of old-school Presbyterianism, Murray's essentially orthodox categories underwent significant modification. Important in this regard were Caleb Rich (1750–1821) and Elhanan Winchester (1751–1797).[7] Born in America, Rich's Universalism evolved from intense inner turmoil over the question of the assurance of salvation. Claiming visionary experiences, Rich was largely responsible for instilling American Universalism with a deep sense of religious experience and the inner dynamic of conversion. Winchester's Universalist arguments resulted in his removal from the Baptists in 1781. A powerful preacher and gifted biblical exegete, Winchester afforded the young denomination theological credibility and gained for it many converts.

However, in the early nineteenth century a more rational, enlightened form of Universalism emerged in contrast to the strongly experiential evangelical piety of its first phase. The architect of this enlightened Universalism was Hosea Ballou (1771–1852).[8] It was Ballou's application of Enlightenment rationalism to the tenets of American Universalism that appealed to Brownson's young and logical mind. Strongly influenced by deistic writings, Ballou's *Treatise on the Atonement* (1805) is a fusion of Chauncy's Arminianism, Rellyan exegesis, and Ethan Allen's *Reason the Only Oracle of Man* (1784). Among the results were a transition from trinitarian to unitarian belief concerning God and Christ, the rejection of a substitutionary view of the atonement in favor of a moral theory that emphasized the atonement as the effect, but not the cause, of God's love, and the denial of any restorative punishment after death. Brownson's writings echoed each of these tenets;

but in his thought they often functioned as foils for the enlightened procla-
mations of the power of human reason.

Revelation and Reason

For the most part, the role of reason in Brownson's early thought is unde-
fined, primarily functioning as a *tabula rasa* upon which the empirical object
impresses itself. As objective truths are communicated to the mind through
the various media, reason functions as the ultimate arbiter of truth. In this
role, Brownson's conception of reason begins to develop. Though Brownson's early epistemology lacks the clarity that would characterize his later
thought, important noetic distinctions begin to emerge.

Fundamental to Brownson's early epistemology is the distinction between belief and knowledge. The two are not to be confused: belief is best
described as opinion, for that which is believed is not empirically and rationally verifiable. Knowledge, however, is empirical and verified by the testimony of the senses. Articles of faith, such as God's existence, his
providence, human accountability, and the future state, are not empirically
and rationally demonstrable and therefore cannot be known. Articles of
faith are only to be believed for the sake of their utility, for the sake of "the
comfort or consolation a belief in a God and a future state may afford the
suffering sons of humanity." But belief is not knowledge. Says Brownson:

> I am a professed christian. I consider the morals, enjoined by Jesus Christ, to be ex-
> cellent; the doctrines he taught, to wit, the character he gave of our heavenly Fa-
> ther and the hope he gave his followers of a future state of happiness, are certainly
> very pleasing to every one who is depressed by adversity or suffering under the nu-
> merous casualties of life. But whether these doctrines are true or not I cannot *abso-
> lutely* know. I may believe, but my belief is not knowledge.[9]

Nor is there much appreciation for the miraculous in Brownson's thought as
a Universalist. He does not deny the biblical miracles, but argues that they
cannot function as evidence of the truth of any doctrine. Moreover, had a
miracle been experienced, it should properly be termed no miracle at all, but
natural, because it would have had to be known empirically for its truth to
be attested. Our attention must be focused on that of which we can possess
certitude, namely, nature and this life. Religion exists primarily for its utility
in this life.

Having relegated religious sentiments to opinion, for they cannot be
known, only believed for their utility, Brownson asks simply for liberality
and graciousness in their exchange. There is little use taxing the intellect or
emotions in pursuit of that which cannot be known with certainty. Toleration is called for in matters of faith. But in matters of knowledge, that is, in

matters pertaining to that which is empirically and rationally verifiable, enlightened reason must be employed in order to clearly discern that which indeed can be known through nature. Brownson's earliest writings often include the urgent call for the use of enlightened reason to alleviate the ills of church and society spawned by ignorance. But in spite of these frequent pleas, it is not until 1829 that Brownson seriously begins to develop his consideration of the role and nature of reason.

"An Essay on Christianity" (1829) signals the beginning of the development of Brownson's early preoccupation with the question of the role of reason.[10] Declaring any doctrine unreasonable that is inconsistent with the natural perception of things, Brownson defines reason as "that faculty by which we perceive the relation of different propositions, and which enables us to determine whether the relation supposed to exist between them, does exist or can exist without destroying either." For example, from the experience of love we know that it is the nature of love to make its object happy. This experience is embodied in the term "love," that is, the determinate idea of the happiness of its object is conveyed by the term "love." If the proposition "Deity loves his creatures" is asserted, it is meant to relay that the Deity delights in his creatures and desires to make them happy. If it is also asserted that "Deity will make these same creatures endlessly miserable," reason can assure us that the latter proposition is false, for it is impossible unless the Deity has been compelled to cease loving. Of this we can be positive because we know through experience the nature of love (212).

Obviously, reason must have some experienced data from which to proceed. But how is this data experienced and what reliability is to be attached to it? Borrowing from Locke, Brownson introduces three levels of evidence from which certitude can be derived: intuitive perception, experience, and the testimony of others. The role of intuitive perception as prior to any process of reasoning is novel in Brownson's thought and indicates the beginning of a movement toward an intuitionism that would soon emerge. Through it we are able to believe our own existence and trust the intelligence of our senses. As such, it supplies certitude for sense experience. Moreover, without any process of reasoning, intuitive perception discloses such first thoughts as the impossibility of the same thing to be and not to be, or that a whole is greater than a part.

The evidence supplied by experience, that is, from the senses, is ranked next in reliability. It comprises whatever is seen, heard, or felt. It is more reasonable to believe that which has been personally experienced through the testimony of one's senses than through the indirect testimony of others. This latter, the testimony of others, is the third form of evidence. It functions as "vicarious empirical evidence."[11] As the alleged testimony of others, it is the least reliable kind of evidence and is to be sharply distinguished from intuitive perception and experience. The Bible, for example, falls under the category of the testimony of others (213).

Though distinguished from the knowledge gained through sense experience, Brownson's notion of intuitive perception remains largely undeveloped. Though it exists prior to any process of reasoning, it is rarely extended to include the realm of belief. During his period as a Universalist, the extension of intuition to the non-empirical is not yet made with any conviction. During his coming Transcendentalist years, Brownson's evolving doctrine of intuition would be shaped largely by the influence of Romantic impulses and becomes the subjective means of immediate appropriation of a non-empirical divine revelation. But at this early stage, intuition remains more closely aligned with the empirical perception of evidence embodied in the natural object, supplying certitude for the reliability of knowledge gained through sense experience. What is responsible for the distinction between intuitive perception and sense experience is the degree of certitude that can be placed in the empirical evidence, not the means through which the non-empirical can be known. But what precisely intuitive perception *is*, what it is in distinction from experience and how it supplies certitude for that experience, is not at all clear at this stage of Brownson's development.

Knowledge, not belief, remains fundamental. The strongest emphasis remains upon the testimony of the senses: "Should I hear a voice from heaven asserting that the two men I now see walking are but one man, I should not believe it, because I have the testimony of my senses...to the contrary" (212). This is not intended to position reason over against the declarations of God, for the voice from heaven also would have been known through the senses; it would have been *heard*. One simply would have chosen the testimony of one sense over that of another. Given the fact that it is not demonstrable that the voice came from God, the plain testimony of sight is the more reliable. With some circularity he continues:

> But how do I know the voice I hear is the voice of God? Do I see God? If I did, and should hear him assert that which contradicted the plain testimony of my senses, I could not believe him. But God has not made such a declaration, and if he be a Being of truth he cannot. But should he make such a declaration, humility might induce us to conclude there was some misapprehension in the case, or some play upon words. Deity might use language in a sense different from what I did, and the apparent falsity of the declaration might result from my misunderstanding the declaration (213).

Be that as it may, revelation from God cannot contradict nature, nor the indubitable testimony of the data of nature as communicated through the senses.

Brownson's treatment of the doctrine of the Trinity in the same essay is an example of the application of his early epistemology to Christian doctrine. Though regarded as fundamental to Christian faith, most trinitarian doctrine, he claims, consists of fruitless attempts to investigate a subject beyond the senses and comprehension. Ignorant of nature and impatient for knowledge, humanity sought after a knowledge of God impossible to attain: "He [humanity] could not submit to the slow and tiresome process of observation and experiment, but with a boldness honorable indeed to the sublimity of his mind, he rashly leaped into the empyreal sphere, determined to survey the throne of the Almighty and from its lofty eminence to give laws to the Universe" (206). But from nature one cannot ascertain that there is a God, much less that God is three persons, Father, Son and Holy Spirit. Nature has never taught this, or at least that part of nature open to human investigation. If the doctrine is true, the evidence of its truth is not to be found among that which can be known. To investigate God in such a way as to prove beyond doubt that he is three persons would require an additional sense, "one which can detect the spiritual world, converse with immaterial existences, tell us what they are, how they are made, and what forms they bear" (207). There is no intuitive perception of God, or of God as triune. While some pretend to have this sense, no one actually does.

Brownson admits that in itself this does not disprove its possibility and is no reason for the for the rejection of the doctrine. But it does not prove its reality either. We are, therefore, under no obligation to believe it and the doctrine is to be relegated to opinion. But if there is something about the doctrine that contradicts known facts, it is to be rejected. The Trinity is not taught by reason and seems to contradict the very first principles of reason. For example, it is impossible for something to be and not to be, or for three to be one, or one to be three. Furthermore, if the trinitarian lodges the protest that words are inadequate to express the divine mystery, it is simply evidence that the doctrine must be unintelligible, unreasonable, or contradictory. Language is adequate to express ideas; if alleged to be inadequate, the idea must have no basis in fact. All that can be tentatively proposed is modalism, that is, that the distinction of persons is actually different displays of the one God (207–08).

But even admitting this runs the risk of committing the error of positing abstractions as first principles from which all else is to be deduced. This is the danger of theory, the love of which is the greatest enemy to the discovery of truth. The love of theory causes all things to be reduced to a few first principles, "that the cause of everything may be given in a word."[12] Rather, reasoning must begin with facts derived from meticulous examination of the things of nature. "Acquaintance with words is useful only as it introduces us to the *things* signified by them."[13] Through discovery of the things of nature, truth itself is discovered, for truth is "a knowledge of facts or simply the observation of things as they are."[14] Thus humanity learns the line of demarcation between what can and cannot be known, learning to place higher value on matters of fact ascertained through the senses than on deductions from theory or hypothesis. Through strict reasoning from facts to laws, the speculative errors of the past can be overcome and a new age of science and progress will result.

Revelation and Nature

During this earliest period of Brownson's career, nature functions as the chief medium of revelation. But in order for reason to appropriate the content of revelation, the truths of which revelation consists must be identified with empirical evidence, for no epistemic means for appropriating a supernatural revelation is alleged. Accordingly, revelation is usually reduced to a mere supplementary role, though at times one finds such a close correlation between revelation and nature that their intimacy would suggest an identification.

Nevertheless, Brownson insists that nature is not revelation; rather, nature is the primary means through which revelation is communicated. Though natural religion and revealed religion differ less in kind than degree, there is a sense in which their distinction allows for the possibility of a supernatural revelation. To employ Brownson's own analogy, revealed or supernatural revelation supplies an increased capacity or added power much in the same way a telescope supplies one's natural eyes with an increased power. Revealed religion is natural religion raised to a higher degree or power.

"The Essayest," one of Brownson's earliest studies as a Universalist, clearly illustrates this phenomenon. The essay begins with a treatment of the relation of revealed religion and natural religion, or revelation and nature. The two are not to be considered in opposition; revealed religion is natural religion enlarged. But one must start with nature, for revelation presupposes knowledge of the natural world:

> Revelation supposes us to be acquainted with the material world—to have obtained all the information the exercises of our natural powers can give; and then bestows itself as a free bounty, as an addition to the fund already accumulated. If we neglect the natural sources of knowledge, if we do not improve the means nature has placed within our reach, we cannot relish the bounties and excellencies of the free gift which our Heavenly Father has made us.[15]

Natural religion is the foundation of the revealed. If our minds had the capacity to take in all the Creator's works in relation to themselves and to God, no greater knowledge, no further revelation, would be necessary. But heaven has kindly supplied that which our natural eyes cannot see.

The frequent mistake of Christians has been to ignore the study of nature and to denounce the acquisition of human wisdom. "Revelation is to the mind what the telescope is to the eye....What should we think of the man who, having once felt the pleasure of looking through it, should put out his natural eyes that he might see only with the telescope?"[16] It is folly to refuse to exercise the natural powers in order to see only by revelation. God's revelation is not made to a brute creation, but to rational beings. The exercise of all the powers they possess is thus demanded.[17]

Brownson's propagation of the doctrines of the Universalists illustrates this "telescopic" view of revelation, whereby revealed religion is regarded as natural religion raised to a higher power. Laboring to prove that the final operation of God's grace will produce the happiness of all humanity, Brownson arranges his arguments in such a way as to demonstrate the consistency of universal salvation with humanity's natural capacity to receive such happiness. "A Sermon on the Salvation of All Men" (1828) serves as an excellent example.[18]

On the objects of his love, Brownson claims, "[God] is determined to bestow...all the happiness, which the nature he gave them is capable of receiving." This assertion entails three questions: "1. What happiness are we capable of receiving? 2. Is it consistent with what we can ascertain of the moral perfections of the Deity, to bestow this happiness? 3. Will he bestow this happiness upon all who are capable of receiving it (150)?" The answer to the first question can be ascertained by determining humanity's original state. The happiness to which humanity can attain is not the happiness of the infinite God. Humanity is finite and the happiness to which it can attain must be proportionately finite. "His happiness may be complete, but it is still the happiness of a man and not of a God." By "complete" is understood all that human nature is capable of bearing, that is, all its original constitution could receive. Moreover, humanity may have fallen, but to restore it to perfection is to give it nothing that does not belong to its original constitution as human:

> Man would then be restored to his moral perfection, and this restoration will present the idea of what is generally supposed to have been his primeval condition. He is endowed with all the faculties requisite to love God and be benevolent to his fellow men. He requires no new principle to enable him to perform all the duties to his God, obligatory on his station and all the offices of justice and humanity due to his brethren (151).

The restoration of humanity's primeval condition and its state of happiness consists simply in the elimination of all external violence and painful sensations endured through the wrongs of humanity and all internal pain of conscience endured as the result of transgressions committed.

Concerning the second question, that is, whether it is consistent with what we can ascertain of the moral perfection of the Deity to bestow this happiness, Brownson asserts that through nature God has revealed of himself all that need be known:

> I presume not to scan the Almighty. All I know of him is what he has revealed of himself. The volume of nature stored with knowledge for all humanity, stands open for the perusal of all who wish to be instructed. On each page is stamped the impress of its Author, in characters so plain that he who runs may read—on leaves so durable that no time or circumstance can efface or render the writing illegible. Here let us read (152).

In the immensity of creation, God's power is read; in its arrangement, his wisdom. God's benevolence is exhibited in the useful, convenient, and pleasurable purposes in which he employs his power and wisdom.

Brownson admits that he cannot ascertain the extent of God's wisdom and power, that is, their infinity cannot be ascertained from nature. Nevertheless, they can be inferred as infinite, for it can be observed from nature that attributes are equal to any purpose of the one who possesses them. If this inference is admitted, others follow:

> If infinite, Deity can have no want, or imperfection. Whatever he desires, his wisdom devises the best means for its accomplishment and his power at once carries it into execution. With these attributes, and the nature which possesses them, he must be perfect, and if perfect, he must be happy. Hence my idea of God is that he is a happy being.—If he be happy himself, it is natural to infer he is delighted with happiness in others, or pleased with the production of happiness in his creatures. This proves him a good Being (153).

It is further observable from nature that those who delight in the misery of others are themselves of an unhappy disposition. People do not afflict their neighbor if they are not unhappy themselves. If follows that the most virtuous are the most happy and the most happy are the most virtuous.

Now a good and happy creation must be more pleasing to God than a wicked and miserable one, for if God is perfectly happy, he must be perfectly virtuous, delighting in goodness and the production of happiness. So creatures are made happy by being made good:

> A creature speaks the language of reason, when it represents God as having "no pleasure in the death of the wicked," "not willing that any should perish," but rather all would turn and live. If God has no pleasure in death, we may suppose he

has pleasure in life, if he delight not in the misery of his children, we may reasonably infer he delights in their felicity (153).

The second question is thus answered in the affirmative.

Before turning to the third question, however, Brownson briefly entertains the problem of sin. Could it be, he asks, that man's sin has "rendered him obnoxious to the justice of God?" Brownson concedes that this is true, but argues that God's justice is itself rooted in and derived from his goodness and is a means that God employs to deliver his goodness:

> Disguise it by what name you please, it will retain the traces of its derivation; it is goodness, or at least so intimately connected with it, that if Deity were not just, he could not be good; nor could he be good if he were not just. The fact is, no being, can be just without being good, nor can one be good without being just. Justice is so far from being opposed to the bestowment of this happiness, that it exerts itself for that purpose, and is one of the principle means Jehovah uses to effect it (154).

God's original design was to create humanity happy. Though we know not the origin of sin, it does not dishonor God that he should execute the sanctions of his law and direct the sinfulness of humanity to an end consistent with that original design.

Having demonstrated inferentially from nature that the bestowing of happiness is consistent with the divine nature, it remains only to show that God will bestow this happiness on all who are capable of receiving it—the content of the third question. Only one of the following, argues Brownson, can be true: "God can bestow this happiness and will not, or would but cannot, or can bestow it and will" (155–56). If one alleges that God could bestow happiness on all, but refuses to do so, God goodness is impeached. If one alleges that God desires to bestow happiness on all, but cannot, God's power is limited. Both of these allegations are tantamount to atheism. Only the last position can be concluded: God can and will bestow this happiness on all.

God cannot govern humanity in a manner inconsistent with the goodness of the divine nature, a goodness one can infer from the goodness of nature. Even if God had created but one individual, the conclusion would be the same. "Had but one man been created, what may we suppose, knowing God to be love, would have been his destination? Happiness to be sure" (156). The same conclusion must be adopted should the figure swell to any number.

Brownson's naturalistic and inferential argument for universal salvation leaves little room for revealed religion. Though supernatural revelation is not denied, it is relegated to a private and inferior role. Nor does Brownson posit a direct and immediate intuition of the existence of God. Such Transcendentalist notions would soon emerge as the result of Romantic influences upon him. At this point the extension of the doctrine of intuition to the non-empirical is only beginning to emerge. But the doctrines of the Universalists remain a matter of belief, not knowledge, and therefore are relegated to the uncertain realm of opinion.

However, "An Essay on Divine Goodness" (1829) indicates the beginning of an important development in young Brownson's thought. In this essay, the clear assertion of an idea implanted into the mind by revelation, but not through the mediation of nature, emerges. The idea is that of the existence of God, which is to be believed not because nature is sufficient to teach it, but because God has revealed himself in Scripture:

> Scripture affirms his existence and nature assures me [that] the existence of such a being clearly accounts for the existence of the objects I admire....I rest the existence of God on this. I see nothing in nature which appears able to originate the idea of God in my mind. But since revelation has informed me there is a God, every thing in nature bears testimony to its truth. Revelation originates the idea, nature *proves* it, but could not of itself have taught it.[19]

Therefore, the senses can only confirm, but not prove, God's existence. The idea of the existence of God is present to the mind prior to the sensation of empirical objects.

While nature cannot prove God's existence, Brownson asserts, with no little confusion, that nature can demonstrate his attributes. An analysis of the flux of nature, of the various effects we discover in the world of matter, leads us to attribute all we see to some cause which precedes its origin, to some cause which has produced it. But it is only the various natural effects that we can truly know. As for the cause, the superior Being, little can be asserted:

> But what this being is, as to his essence or substance of his existence we know not, we cannot ascertain, therefore it is useless to inquire. How this being exists we know not, and his physical connexion with the universe it is impossible for us to explain. We can affirm nothing of the secret power which is every where to work, for we know nothing. All we can affirm is that we see various events transpire, and various changes in the natural world constantly taking place.[20]

Though it is easy to conclude that the cause producing the greatness, beauty, and systematic arrangement of the universe must be powerful and intelligent, this can only be believed, not known. All that is known is that the world is, for its beginning has never been seen.

Nor can nature prove the existence of God: "Many a sincere christian believes he can prove from *nature* the existence of a God. He may, but I cannot. What is nature? Nature is whatever is....Nature can prove nothing separate from itself; and should it prove the existence of a God, that God would either be nature or a part of nature. This is the same as atheism."[21] The universe cannot travel outside of itself to prove the existence of a deity, who to be God must be by definition independent of the universe. Knowledge is of nature alone and our concern is to be only with that which can be known. Christianity is designed to improve the moral lot of humanity and humanity has been equipped with the natural faculties necessary to receive all that in justice God can require. Therefore, for revelation to be known, to be normative, it must come naturally, otherwise it is unintelligible and cannot be proved to be from God.

Unfortunately, Brownson's argument is equally valid with respect to the doctrine of universal salvation, for neither has the end of time been seen. Brownson's increasing difficulties with the Universalists and his movement away from them is two-fold and now becomes evident: First, he virtually denies any divine revelation or existence of the supernatural. Secondly, the conclusions of his naturalistic method are not conducive to arguing the final complete restoration of all humanity. But clearly he is not yet teaching an immediate intuition of a supernatural revelation. Nor is his Lockean notion of intuitive perception epistemologically operative in relation to the idea of God. Indeed, the idea is communicated to the mind through the empirical evidence of Scriptural propositions. Nevertheless, this convoluted essay hints at the emergence of a notion of primitive revelation supernaturally communicated and immediately intuited by the knowing subject. Though the Enlightenment reduction of the scope of the intelligible to the empirical is everywhere present in Brownson's thought as a Universalist minister, such seemingly misplaced themes anticipate later developments. The relation of revelation and history further manifests these themes.

Revelation and History

It is not to be assumed that the category of history functions in Brownson's Universalist thought in any decisive fashion. Though some notions of revelations progressively disclosed in history occur sporadically, his writings as a Universalist display a certain Enlightenment disdain for the past. Often history is referred to negatively, as exemplary of what goes wrong as the result of a preoccupation with heavenly worlds to which humanity has no access. In contrast, the dawning age is to be the new and liberating age of science and progress.

Nevertheless, Brownson pays some attention to history and occasionally affords it a more positive role. For example, his sermon on Revelation 5.1 ("And I saw in the right hand of him that sat on the throne a book written within and on the backside, sealed with seven seals.") deals with history as a continual disclosure of the knowledge of God insofar as humanity is ready to receive it.[22] This fascinating example of an Enlightenment exegesis of biblical text identifies the breaking of the seals and the disclosure of the content of the sealed book with humanity's search for the knowledge of God as revealed in nature. Accordingly, humanity becomes gradually prepared to accept increasing manifestations of God's design in nature.

The sages of antiquity, despite all their effort, were only able to see the name of God traced on the outside of the book, that is, on the outside of nature. They could not discover what God had written within, for God had yet to disclose it: "They scanned the various operations of nature; they soared with genius through regions of ether; they delved with knowledge in the mines of understanding. Vain alike the flight and the descent...and they were compelled to retire ignorant as they commenced (1)!" Though God could have created humanity with complete knowledge, he choose to create not a god, nor an angel:

> He made him MAN, gave him all the powers and faculties necessary to secure him that rank in the scale of being for which he designed him. He placed him here, surrounded him with a variety of objects to attract his attention and engage his pursuit. He subjected him to disappointments, and evils of different kinds, that he might be led to the development of his own powers and to the ascertaining of his own resources (2).

Whatever else God would give this creature would be additional manifestations of benevolence, gratuities that would add nothing to the natural constitution of humanity. In short, God created humanity as progressive, susceptible of improvement one step at a time.

Accordingly, the opening of the book, the breaking of the seals, is gradual. With each lesson learned, humanity is given another. This is its nature; to deny it is to retard the race:

> There seems to have crept into the minds of men, an idea, pregnant with deleterious consequences, that in religion, man has arrived at a stand; that in this interesting science we are to attempt no further improvement. The effect of such a sentiment is to paralyze the human mind, and render dormant all the active powers of man. Nature, providence and grace never said to man in his religious career, "Hitherto shalt thou come, but no further" (2).

But the age of science has arrived and it is science that elevates the human intellect. As the powers of the human intellect advance and the great principles of nature are discovered, humanity receives a religion more correct, exalted, and beneficial in its practical implications.

Prior to 1829, this is the extent of the role of history in Brownson's thought. Man is created a progressive being and given the powers and means to enact this progression. "Creation was contrived to assist him; the several parts of which it is composed, the good and the evil, the pleasure and the pain, all were adapted to this purpose" (3). Having arrived at a point of unprecedented scientific discovery and development, humanity is poised to enter a new age of unrivaled truth, beauty, and knowledge. There remains, however, a great deal of work to accomplish. The world has been overrun with static religious systems and the people remain in the clutches of an unscrupulous clergy unwilling to relinquish its authoritarian pretensions. Only freedom of thought will deliver the people from their bondage.

Revelation and Scripture

As is the case with history, Scripture does not function as a major category in Brownson's Universalist thought. Reason, not Scripture, is the bar of truth. Nonetheless, out of his doctrine of Scripture emerges the notion of a primitive revelation corresponding to the idea of a revelation disclosed progressively in history.

As indicated above, Brownson classifies the Bible under the epistemological category of the testimony of others. As such, its evidence is of the least reliable. It cannot authorize belief in what contradicts intuitive perception or experience. In "An Essay on Christianity,"[23] Brownson writes: "A thing which contradicts our intuitive perception or our experience, we should at once pronounce false....What contradicts reason or experience, our intuitive perception, or our own knowledge we are to reject, Bible or no Bible: what is beyond our reason or experience, may or may not be true" (214–15). Indeed, that the Bible is the word of God we have only human testimony to insure. While those to whom the Bible was given possessed greater evidence of its teachings, at this late date in history only the testimony of others remains. The testimony of the Bible cannot be allowed when there is greater evidence gained to the contrary. Nor do miracles prove anything. They are no evidence of the truth of any doctrine (226–29).

However, the Bible also can contain that which is beyond, but not necessarily opposed to, reason. In all such cases the Bible may be regarded as infallible. The idea of the existence of God is exemplary. Though the senses can confirm God's existence through nature, they cannot prove it nor originate the idea. Likewise, that which is currently beyond reason may be proved to be consistent with nature at some later date:

> Should it be asserted that a part is equal to a whole, that black is white, or that pain is pleasure, we may pronounce such assertions unfounded. But should it be asserted

> that Jesus Christ rose from the dead, we cannot pronounce it false, because we do
> not know that it was true, we know not but there is a law of nature which may pro-
> duce such a result (214).

Again, nature could affirm the assertion, but could not originate it. Similarly, Brownson teaches an inspiration of the Bible "by suggestion," meaning
that a spirit of ardour or disposition came upon the minds of Jesus and the
apostles and suggested that which is to be communicated. Therefore, the inspired mind feels a certain impulse. Not all of the Bible is inspired, however.
It contains many errors and contradictions. Finally, only the New Testament doctrines of Jesus, that is, his moral teachings, are inspired (218–26).

By 1829, many Universalists were growing increasingly disturbed with
Brownson's insistence that nature is incapable of originating the idea of
God's existence. Though Brownson's frequent appeals to Scripture pacified
some, it was becoming clear that his denial of nature's ability to teach the
existence of God was tantamount to relegating the existence of God to the
realm of opinion. If nature cannot teach it, it cannot be known, only believed.

One particular Universalist, W.I. Reese, charged Brownson with atheism for allowing only a natural inspiration of Scripture, for not allowing
enough of Scripture to be inspired, and for denying that nature teaches the
existence of God. To the first charge, Brownson asserts that humanity is not
dependent upon an inspiration for its ideas of God, but only upon a revelation. Inspiration is a holy power present in nature generally; it can illumine
individuals in an extraordinary, though not supernatural, fashion. This does
not delimit inspiration because the extent of the natural is unknown. Moreover, those persons inspired were natural in all respects and the knowledge
they gained was communicated through natural means.[24]

To the second charge, Brownson points out that no Universalist believes all of Scripture to be inspired, the difference is simply how much.
Brownson claims, though does not demonstrate, that only the New Testament doctrines are inspired; the Old Testament is largely superseded. But
this does not prove atheism. Finally, to the third charge, Brownson reasserts
that nature does not teach God's existence. It is necessary to distinguish between God as a being separate from nature and a "Mighty Energy" that per-
vades all of nature. This energy is indeed God, but we are not informed of
such by nature:

> By the term God we understand a Being separate from nature, intelligent, inde-
> pendent, who originated nature and exerts a voluntary control over it. By the power
> or energy which expressions we use, we mean nothing more than the great active
> principle we every where see exerted. This power is indeed God, but nature could
> not teach us this fact, nature cannot teach his personality and his voluntary control

over the universe. This distinction is important....This mighty Power or Energy is taught by nature, and every Atheist may admit it. But, the other ideas, which we believe are essential to the term God, as all Theists understand the term, we teach are learned not from nature, but from revelation (368).

All humans in every age believe in the existence of God, but not in a philosophical sense which nature has provided, but in the sense in which revelation teaches God's existence.

While it is true that only the New Testament doctrines are inspired, humanity believed in the existence of God well before the New Testament was written. This is to say that the Bible and revelation are not synonymous terms. The revelation occurred well prior to the writing of the New Testament:

> We consider revelation, a communication made from God to man, and made in the early ages of this world. Being made before the dispersion of mankind, it was easily carried with them as they wandered from each other, and thus became spread over the earth. The sacred books of all nations exhibit some traces of it, though the most pure and authentick accounts of it are found in the Jewish and Christian scriptures. The doctrinal parts of the New Testament teach what this revelation was (369).

Finally then, the New Testament doctrines are not themselves revelation, but authentic records of a primitive revelation.

Brownson presents five reasons for positing this early revelation: (1) In the earliest writings of humanity there are notices of a Being called God, which could not be learned from nature alone. (2) If the idea of God is not derived from a contemplation of nature, it must either be a self-evident proposition or taught by revelation. Too many have doubted God's existence to assert it as self-evident; it must, therefore, be the result of revelation. (3) All religions point to a common origin, even in regard to particulars that could not have been taught by nature. (4) All Divines, ancient and modern, have taught it. (5) Every moral precept and doctrine recorded in the New Testament predates the New Testament by hundreds of years. To deny this is to deny that the Christian doctrines were taught by revelation, which is finally to deny Christianity itself (369–370).

This early or primitive revelation is the closest to what may be termed a supernatural revelation in Brownson's Universalist thought. Though he seems almost reluctant to affirm it, he employs it to assure his readers that he is not guilty of atheism, of denying the existence and revelation of God. But in much the same way that nature confirms but does not prove the idea of God, the New Testament doctrines confirm but do not prove the primitive revelation. That such a revelation had been imparted is posited as Brownson's defense against charges of atheism, but he has not posited any epistemological means whereby the revelation had been or can be known. Its relegation to the distant past is, therefore, understandable.

Revelation and Jesus

The role of Jesus in Brownson's Universalist thought is relatively minor. As with history and Scripture, Jesus functions as a less important medium of objective truths communicated to the reason. Nor is Christianity considered a new revelation, but only an intensification of the natural. Accordingly, the role of Jesus is less integral than the chief medium of objective truths, namely, nature. Yet, some significance can be found in Jesus' role as supreme teacher of moral truth.

According to Brownson, the mission of Jesus was not to reconcile God to humanity, for God already loved humanity. Therefore, Brownson rejects any notion of propitiation, vicarious atonement, or imputed righteousness. He finds it repulsive to believe that God would declare a sinner righteous without actually making him righteous. Rather, the mission of Jesus was to advance humanity through the communication and repetition of truth. Jesus did not attempt to advance humanity through any supernatural means, but through "a simple operation, differing in degree, not in kind, from the labors of any reformer." Jesus' mission was to reform humanity, but his age misunderstood him and put him to death:

> It should be born in mind, that Jesus of Nazareth, was one of those benevolent individuals who are far in advance of the age in which they appear. The true nature of his mission was but imperfectly understood by his immediate disciples, and the succeeding age, who incorporated…the pompous absurdities of prevailing systems of religion and philosophy, soon lost sight of their teacher, and retained nothing more of the Jewish Reformer than the name. His pretended disciples soon raised him from a man to an angel, from that to a demi-god, and at length a god. Thus deified, he must have a work equal in magnitude to his supposed divinity.[25]

The mission of Jesus was simply to reform the world through exemplary and natural means. Truth is found in what he taught, not in his person. The New Testament displays him as the greatest and best reformer, as the master teacher of truth, and therefore to be imitated. But the teachings of Jesus recorded in the New Testament did not originate with him. He taught nothing radically new, nothing that was not previously true. He added nothing to nature. Jesus simply proclaimed and gave witness to the eternal truth inherent in nature. Though his teachings may be applicable to a future state, no new principle was added to any other world but this.

Only briefly does Brownson incorporate the role of Jesus with the notion of a primitive revelation: "But as this revelation became corrupted by all nations, so that it was nearly useless, about two thousand years ago, God sent his own Son and his disciples to separate what was true from what was false, and to tell us plainly what is truth."[26] Jesus was the great reformer and is to be imitated because of his knowledge and reassertion of the truth that God revealed long ago. This repetition of the primitive revelation is embodied in the New Testament teachings, which are to be considered inspired. But this is the extent of any relation of Jesus to an early revelation. As doctrines of history and incarnation would later become crucial to his thought, the incorporation of the role of Jesus with primitive revelation likewise would become vital. But a major reconstruction of this thought as a whole would first take place. Brownson's position as a Universalist simply mirrored the Enlightenment reduction of religion to morality, and the role of Jesus to moral exemplar and teacher of truths.

Transition: Free Inquiry and Early Unitarianism

Brownson's refusal to believe in reason's capacity or ability to know God led to frequent accusations of atheism and infidelity from his Universalist peers. Tiring of the bitter doctrinal infighting among them and craving intellectual freedom, Brownson tended increasingly toward social radicalism. Finally, despairing of religion itself, Brownson left the Universalists in late 1829 to affiliate with the "Free Enquirers," a utopian and agnostic movement of social reform led by the radical communitarians Francis Wright (1795–1852) and Robert Dale Owen (1771–1858). In a letter written in 1834 to the Reverend Edward Turner, Brownson relates his Universalist experience:

> I thought it [Universalism] rational, taught by the Bible and calculated to do good. With this connection I became a Universalist preacher. But when I reasoned I leaned to infidelity, and it was only when I attempted to take things on trust that I was a believer. My feelings were religious. But soon I found that all my religious feelings were laughed at by my brethren, and that to be pious was to be in their estimation a great fool. Alone with them they were unbelievers, with them in public they were found to be…persecutors of infidels. The effect of such associates on a mind like mine especially in the state it then was, you can easily imagine. My religion grew less, my unbelief greater, stronger. I struggled to believe, but in vain.[27]

Brownson would exert his energies elsewhere.

Each having failed in communitarian experiments, Wright and Owen helped organize the Workingmen's Party. First organized in Philadelphia in 1827 following labor strikes in the building trades, the party was organized in New York two years later.[28] Brownson had first heard Wright lecture in October, 1829, in Utica, New York, and wrote favorably of her in the *Gospel Advocate and Impartial Investigator*, further alienating him from the Universalists.[29] Though he shied away from her utopianism, it is clear that her views on the need for more general education largely coincided with his.[30] Both were Lockean empiricists and hence ascribed to the Lockean educational theory which taught that the mind of the newborn child is a *tabula rasa* and is formed solely by empirical impressions upon it. Moreover, both possessed utilitarian conceptions of morality and both despised religious sectarianism and clericalism.[31]

But Brownson was never an avowed atheist.[32] Though assailed by doubt and skepticism, he refused to abandon religion altogether. From the pages of *The Free Enquirer* he writes to the Universalists:

> I do not renounce my former religious belief, nor do I denounce the denomination to which I was attached. I but say, I am no longer to appear the advocate of any sect, nor of any religious faith. I am too ignorant to preach Universalism or any other religious sentiment; and I *will* be too honest to preach that which I do not know. I become an enquirer after truth in the field of knowledge....I wish to be simply an observer of nature for my creed, and a benefactor of my brethren for my religion.[33]

Brownson's resignation from preaching any religious creed was genuine and honest and his desire to benefit humanity sincere, but he could not long do without religion. Consequently, his affiliation with the movement was short lived. Concluding the impossibility of divorcing religion and reform, he arrived at his lifelong principle that Christianity constitutes the principle of all social and moral reform. Though not yet identifying that principle with a supernatural element, Brownson could write:

> I remained a skeptic about a year, my religious feelings came up, my wishes for a moral Reform were not satisfied by skepticism, which I soon saw was powerless for good. Christianity presented itself to me as an element of Reform. As such I lived upon it, and began to preach it. I began then to study it in a new light, and the result has been a firm conviction of its truth.[34]

Accordingly, Brownson assumed the name Unitarian, "first as a defense against the attacks of the Universalists, who still treated me as any infidel, and because I liked the major part of the Unitarian sentiment."[35] Settling in Ithica, he resumed preaching, established and edited *The Philanthropist*, contributed to the *Christian Register*, and soon accepted the position of pastor of the Unitarian Society of Walpole, New Hampshire.

Major influences were at work on Brownson's mind during this period, shedding the new light in which he resumed his study of Christianity. These influences resulted in a reassessment of the nature and role of reason, and of the positing of revelation and reason as intimately related. It was during his time at Walpole that he first began reading the Saint-Simonians, followers of Claude Henry Count de Saint-Simon (1760–1825), a French philosopher who advocated an allegedly new system of society, rooted in love for the poor and lowly, that would eliminate all inequalities in the distribution of property and power. But Channing's writings were even more important. Channing's elevated view of humanity's freedom, goodness, and rationality as "likeness to God" served Brownson by bringing God and the human in closer proximity through a predication of similarity of divine and human attributes. Of Channing, Brownson wrote:

> To *his* writings, and to the conversation of *one* who deserves to be more extensively known—one who has sustained rational Christianity for seventeen years in the midst of every opposition, removed from nearly all sympathy with his brethren, and at the sacrifice of nearly every comfort except a calm temper, an active mind, and a warm heart—I am indebted for my escape from infidelity.[36]

The writings of the Saint-Simonians appealed to him as a means of positing Christianity as the principle of social reform. In distinction from the "Free Enquirers," religion was afforded a positive role in human social endeavor.

The pages of *The Philanthropist*, however, indicate that the influence of Channing was most important to Brownson in the early 1830s. Channing's lofty view of the human soul manifests itself in Brownson's idea of an inner voice testifying to the reality of God as father, as the benevolent and moral ruler of the universe. This idea signals the beginning of a transition from a doctrine of revelation as identified with the external object and with knowledge in distinction from belief, to one of revelation as embodied in the subject and identified with consciousness or feelings.

Brownson's letter, "To the Rev. Wm. Wisner," exemplifies this transition. Wisner, a Presbyterian minister, had represented Unitarianism as the "doctrine of the devil." With a calm uncharacteristic of his Universalist writings and perhaps in imitation of Channing, Brownson responds with a involved defense of Unitarianism, based upon his newly found notions of an inner revelation and the likeness of divine and human nature. No longer appealing to reason as simply a faculty of critical judgment but as constituting humanity's likeness to God, Brownson urges that it is each individual's duty to decide correctly in matters of religion. Reason is "that faculty which unites the present with the past and future, which links earth to heaven, and man to the Deity." Furthermore, revelation plays a role in the discovery of the truths of religion:

> I do not pretend that reason could have discovered all the truths of religion, but revelation can discover them only to our reason....It assists reason, but without reason it were useless. I use reason to determine whether God has given me a revelation; what that revelation is....I do not determine *a priori* what God should reveal,

and then infer what he has revealed; but I do exercise my reason in interpreting his word.[37]

Revelation and reason have moved into close proximity, for reason has become the natural condition for the possibility of revelation.

Moreover, Scripture, itself a faithful record of revelation made by God to humanity, is to be read according to this inner light, that is, not according to the letter, but according to the spirit. It is here that the inspired doctrines of Jesus are discovered, doctrines concerning God's nature as father, our likeness to God, and our consequent duty. The inner revelation from God to the human soul confirms the truth of Jesus' teachings.

Among the attributes of the Deity, Brownson continues, are God's eternality, intelligence, spiritualness, and oneness. As eternal, God is "the universal principle of vitality—existence itself." As intelligence, God is "not a blind necessity…[but] intelligence itself; an incomprehensible mind, that acts with a plan,…the source of all intelligence." While God's spiritualness cannot be defined, it is "something which the soul perceives and with which it communes.…It is nothing which the outward senses can detect, but it is no less real." Finally, God's oneness is demanded by the oneness of nature's design and by the necessity of fastening our hearts on a single being rather than a confusing multiplicity of gods.[38]

The sum of these attributes is the fatherhood of God. It is as father that God is known and experienced:

> I prefer to contemplate him as Father. I call him my Father, and I mean something more by this term than that he is my creator. He created the wood of which my writing desk is made, but it were absurd to pronounce him its Father. But I can approach him as a Father, and am commanded to be a follower of him as a dear child. It is in this view that I discover the worth of the Divine character. Here I discover an intimate connexion between the human and the Divine natures. Here God appears not in the dread character of a sovereign; here I see him not as a stern unfeeling tyrant, a vindictive judge; but as my Father.[39]

God appears to humanity not as an opposite, but in likeness of nature communicated to the soul by an inner revelation.

This crucial development in Brownson's thought signals a confusion that would plague him in coming years. It is not clear, to Brownson or his reader, whether reason is to be identified with revelation, or merely with the epistemological means whereby revelation is recognized and appropriated. It would seem that the latter is for the most part true in the pages of *The Philanthropist*, published in 1831 and 1832. During these years the so-called "inner revelation" functions primarily as an enabling power or light, as an epistemological principle of illumination, a subjective means of immediate appropriation of an objective revelation. But this would not long remain the case. An identification of revelation and subjectivity, or more specifically, of revelation and the spontaneous reason would soon occur as Brownson would move into a brief, but critically determinative, period of subjectivism.

CHAPTER TWO

Revelation and the Intuiting Subject (1833–1836)

A STUDY OF Brownson's conception of revelation during the years 1833 through 1836 manifests considerable ambiguity and change from his previous position as a Universalist minister. These years represent a period of transition and increasing philosophical maturity in his intellectual development. Corresponding to a Romantic intuitionism, Brownson's notion of revelation becomes increasingly dependent upon a newly developed epistemological principle, namely, the doctrine of the religious sentiment. Whereas revelation had been dependent upon empirical evidence, it now becomes dependent upon his theory of the intuiting subject.

This period also represents the beginning of the influence of Victor Cousin (1792–1867) and other contemporary French thinkers upon Brownson's thought. While Cousin's influence is not yet as clear and decisive as that of Benjamin Constant (1767–1830), Cousin would emerge as the most important philosophical influence on Brownson during his entire Protestant period. Brownson began his reading of Cousin and Constant, as well as other members of the French Eclectic school, in 1833 and began to interpret even the revered Channing through their categories.

Through the influence of Channing, Brownson had developed the idea of an inner voice or revelation that began his movement away from a strict empiricism. Though Brownson never gives up the possibility of an external revelation, Constant's theme of the religious sentiment becomes so pervasive that for all intents and purposes Brownson's understanding of revelation during this period may be regarded as a form of subjectivism.

However, it is precisely at this point that the ambiguity in Brownson's thought shows itself. For example, considerable misunderstanding can occur if Brownson's different uses of the word and concept "reason" are not made clear. In the earlier articles of this period "reason" refers to the rational and reflective principle of subjectivity secondary to the religious sentiment, a distinction derived from Cousin, and similar to the meaning given the term by Brownson as a Universalist. In the later articles "reason" is itself the religious sentiment, in correspondence to an epistemological intuitionism. The rational and reflective principle is then termed the "understanding."[1] Complicating the matter is the use of the word "belief" in relation to both the religious sentiment and the rational principle.[2] Moreover, Cousin's concept of the reason as impersonal, and therefore consisting of more than a private religious sentiment of sorts, is also beginning to emerge in Brownson's thought. This concept, however, remains vague during these years, lending only further confusion.

The major portion of this second chapter furthers the study of Brownson's doctrine of revelation through continued use of the categories of reason, nature, history, Scripture, and Jesus. These sections are preceded by the relevant historical contextualization and a separate section dealing with the religious sentiment. The last section deals with Brownson's growing reservations with the subjectivism he comes to recognize in the thought of others, as well as in his own position. As such, this last section forms the transition to Brownson's period of attempted synthesis, dealt with in Chapter Three.

Unitarianism

From the time of his installation as pastor of the Walpole, New Hampshire, congregation in 1832 until his conversion to Roman Catholicism in 1844, Brownson participated fully in the intellectual fermentation that characterized Unitarianism during the antebellum period. Formed as a denomination in 1825, Unitarianism has its roots in the rationalist reaction to the religious enthusiasm of the Great Awakening of the previous century. Chauncy is most often pointed to as the leading figure of the reaction and his *Seasonable Thoughts* (1743) its original expression. Characterized by the Enlightenment virtues of reason and objectivity, the movement spawned by Chauncy's rationalist reaction consisted of firm anti-revivalism and anti-pietism. The dissenters rejected the emphasis upon a religion of the heart and the experience of conversion as central to the Christian life. Rather, they espoused commitment to a life-long process of calm and objective reflection, dedicated to the moral rectitude of humanity. It also shared with the Universalists a common enemy, namely, rigid predestinarian Calvinism.[3]

Doctrinally, the movement is best characterized by its anti-Calvinist Arminianism, emphasizing confidence in reason as expressed through its belief in the free will of humanity, and tending toward universalism through an emphasis upon the benevolence of God toward all his creatures. The movement took on its Unitarian character largely through the influence of the English anti-trinitarian Joseph Priestly (1733–1804). Arriving in America in 1794, Priestley's Socinian Unitarianism was well received by many of the rationalists and led to the establishment in Philadelphia in 1796 of the first church to call itself Unitarian.

It remained for Channing, however, to give the classic expression of American Unitarianism in his 1819 sermon "Unitarian Christianity." Emphasizing the unity and perfections of the divine character, and teaching an Arian rather than Socinian view of Jesus, Channing succeeded in providing the unifying definitions and impetus needed for the movement to emerge as a denomination. In October of 1825 the American Unitarian Association was formed.

It is important not to over-emphasize the Enlightenment rationalism and anti-revivalist roots of the Unitarians to the extend of ignoring their reliance on the inner self, however. As Channing's influential 1828 sermon "Likeness to God" reveals, antebellum Unitarianism was anything but a cold and abstract rationalist ideology. Robinson writes:

> Rationalism, in other words, goes only so far in explaining Unitarianism.... The Unitarians used reason primarily to liberate themselves from Calvinism, and although they continued to search for rational bases for their belief, the real grounding of their religion was in the emotions. This reliance on the emotions or "affections" had both an inward and an outward manifestation. Inwardly, the Unitarians of this period stressed devotionalism and religious meditation much in the tradition of Christian pietism. By contrast, a stress on the importance of the affections, defined in terms of duty, social responsibility, and Christian love, focused Unitarian energies outward toward both social reform and further denominational organization.[4]

This is especially true of the 1830s when the influence of Romanticism began to be felt among the Boston intellectuals, particularly in the emergence of American Transcendentalism.

Likewise, Brownson's thought during this period reflects both the importance of the inner self and the beginning of the influence of Romanticism upon his thought. As Butler claims, from this time forward, "Brownson never wavered in his conviction that humans have an inborn spiritual element to their being."[5] Indeed, that "spiritual element" becomes a foundational epistemological principle for Brownson during this period.

Romanticism, of course, is notoriously difficult to define, but the identification of the following Romantic themes and impulses will suffice for this study, keeping in mind that in some distinction from European models, Romanticism in America is almost invariably operative in furthering the ideals of freedom and progress:[6] (1) The role of *intuition* is stressed as the epistemological foundation through which the infinite totality of life is known. The unity of the infinite and the finite is, for example, intuitive. The mind is not a *tabula rasa*, but an active force constituted by "facts of consciousness," that is, *a priori* ideas that are regarded as necessarily valid. (2) An idealistic, metaphysical stress on the *unity* of all things is emphasized, according to which the attempt to reconcile and harmonize such dualities as subject/object and infinite/finite is made. For example, the divine is not understood to be extrinsic to nature as the Enlightenment tendency toward deism would construe it, but inclusive of life and nature. The finite is understood as possessing the infinite and divine at its core, resulting in a longing for the finite to express itself infinitely. (3) *Nature* is conceived as a living organic whole, clothed in beauty and majesty. An immanent "Spirit" is felt to be at work in all things. Rather than a closed mechanical system, nature is regarded as a creative process of increasing diversification, the organic unity of which is intuitive. (4) *History* takes on increased significance. The infinite is also understood to be active in time. Therefore, continuity, development, progress, and tradition are emphasized. No longer is history important only for what was common and universal to the past, for each age has its own intrinsic excellence. Humanity inescapably belongs to history. (5) The quest for unity is manifest in *community*, again, conceived as organic. Community is not merely the collectivity of individual wills, but an arena for the activity of the infinite. Authority is often emphasized as the means by which the organic unity of the community is held together.

The 1830s was a decade of dynamic intellectual activity and controversy. After two years at Walpole, Brownson was installed in May, 1834, as pastor of the First Congregational Church (Unitarian) in Canton, Massachusetts. Brownson's proximity to Boston and involvement with the Boston intelligentsia, who were largely responsible for importing and propagating Romantic themes and impulses, was a boon to his own intellectual development. Freed from his rather naive use of Lockean categories by Cousin's critique of British empiricism, Brownson's thought begins to take on a depth and maturity largely lacking heretofore.

The Religious Sentiment

While at Walpole, Brownson turned his attention to Constant's five volume *Religion, Considered in Its Origin, Its Forms, and Its Development* (1824). From this work, Brownson derived the concept of a religious sentiment common to all humanity and constituting the "fundamental law of human nature."[7] Brownson's whole-hearted adaptation of this concept represents the completion of a shift from an identification of revelation with the objective and empirical to the subjective and intuitional.

The religious sentiment is an intuition, an immediate and direct revelatory influence of God upon the human soul. As the soul bears a real likeness to God, so religion is an influence of spirit upon spirit, a sharing of attributes differing only in degree, not in kind. Therefore, religion is not a deduction of reason, but a sentiment, an inspiration:

> It is the poetry of the soul. It enables the soul to call up and solve by a sort of intuition, all the great problems relating to God and to human destiny, and to solve them, not by reasoning, not by reflection, but by faith, sincere, and so firm that it is to the soul like knowledge, only a knowledge of which it can give no account. It opens the eyes of the soul, and gives it power to see truths of the utmost importance to the conduct of life, but to see them as sentiments, as influences to be felt, rather than as distinct doctrines.[8]

The religious sentiment is the voice of God, the breathings of his spirit into the human soul. "It is something within us, not dependent on our reason, immediate and irresistible in its action. No argument creates it, none can destroy it. It is natural to us, we feel it, know it."[9] Man is religious by nature: "He is determined to it [religion] by an interior sentiment, by a fundamental law of his being, a law invariable, eternal, indestructible."[10] The religious sentiment supplies the spiritual person with a new energy, an inspiration directing all the affairs of life.

The concept of the religious sentiment supplies Brownson with the impetus for a bold indictment of the empiricism that had characterized his own thought as a Universalist. He writes:

> We are heartily sick of the frigid philosophy of our times, and especially of our own country. There is a coldness in our religious and philosophical speculations, that chills the heart, and freezes up the very life blood of the soul…. The last century and the first fourth of the present, have been distinguished by the progress made in the physical sciences, and in the application of them to the purposes of life. Men's thoughts have been turned almost exclusively to external nature…. [T]hey have been so engrossed with that world, so delighted with the discoveries they have made in it, that they have almost entirely neglected or denied the existence of that mind, without which it were to us as though it were not. They have been so occupied, so filled with the material world, that they have materialized everything.[11]

So also with respect to religion; all is outward and objective. God is placed at an infinite distance from the human soul and clothed with a materiality that prevents him from reaching the human heart. But the religious sentiment reveals the opposite. God is to be found by turning within.

Specifically, the religious sentiment consists of three distinct intuitions. It reveals the existence of God, the immortality of the soul, and the moral

accountability of humanity. Those who deny these deny no mere propositions, but their own nature, for their intuitions lie at the very root of human
existence.[12]

The religious sentiment reveals the existence of God:

> God is all we can conceive of the great, the wise, the good, the beautiful and the
> true. His moral character is the union of all the perfections. His energy created and
> sustains all worlds and beings, his wisdom controls all events; his bounty provides
> for all that live. He is the mind, the soul of the universe, the mighty Spirit...[13]

This is the idea that the truly religious person has of God. This person has
the ability to turn the mind in upon itself, to hear the voice of God within
and discover a kindred spirit with the divine. In this consists the dignity of
human nature. Hence, to truly worship God is not to degrade human nature,
nor to simply engage in outward acts. It rather consists of the submission,
love, and reverence that seeks to become like God, perfect as he is perfect.

The religious sentiment reveals the immortality of the soul: "We feel
that we are something, that our being has some object, that we are heirs of
an inheritance incorruptible and eternal in the heavens." By virtue of this
intuition "we rise in conscious worth; we rise to the abode of spirit, and borrow some of the sunshine of that fairer and better world to tinge with loveli-
ness that one in which we dwell." Those who believe they will live on are
sustained in this present life. One need not fear death; one need not fear
that one's lifelong efforts will be abandoned:

> I may die before I have finished my present study. But I can take it up hereafter
> where I left it off.... [N]o one, therefore, need fear to engage in any pursuit after
> knowledge. Death will only be the delay of a night's sleep and we shall rise in the
> morning invigorated by rest, prepared to go forward with increasing ardor and ever
> enlarging power.[14]

The intuition of the immortality of the soul finds its highest value in the
motivation and assurance that the pursuit of knowledge, the work done in
this life, shall always continue.

Finally, the religious sentiment reveals the moral accountability of humanity: Moral conduct does not bear the immediate relation to the acts and
development of the intellect as commonly assumed. Moral acts are not inferred from intellectual judgments:

> One may know what righteousness is, may believe the truth, be able to defend it by
> arguments of irresistible beauty and strength, but it does not follow from this...that
> he obeys the truth and is righteous. He may know what it is to love his neighbor,
> may believe that he ought to love him, but who would infer from this that he does
> love him?[15]

Proper moral conduct is rooted in a direct appeal to the religious sentiment common to all. Morality is not first of all utilitarian, but based on a "primitive idea" that is part of human nature itself. It reveals that eternal law of justice, which is anterior to all other laws, and from which all other laws derive their authority.[16]

In summary, Brownson finds in Constant's concept of the religious sentiment a dynamic impetus for expanding his notion of an "inner revelation," derived primarily from Channing. Though the terminology had at times suggested otherwise, the intimate identification of revelation with the intuiting subject entailed by the concept of the religious sentiment was not nearly so pronounced in Brownson's previous concept of an "inner revelation." While the latter signaled a crucial development, it was primarily an epistemological principle or means whereby an objective revelation was appropriated. The religious sentiment, however, is itself the voice of God, a revelation made to the human soul and consisting of a specified threefold content. As such, it becomes the ruling principle of his thought.

Because of the primacy of the doctrine of the religious sentiment, Brownson's thought undergoes a significant shift from a Lockean epistemology and mechanistic view of nature to an emphasis upon the dynamic activity of the reason as it shapes and directs all areas of human endeavor. This theme expands as Brownson gradually incorporates Cousin's view of the reason as impersonal and spontaneous. In keeping with this emphasis, the discussion below begins with a more detailed treatment of the relation of revelation and reason before turning to the relation of revelation to nature, history, Scripture, and Jesus.

Revelation and Reason

It is clear from the above that the doctrine of the religious sentiment constitutes the chief epistemological principle of Brownson's thought during this period. Accordingly, the treatment of the relation of revelation and reason has already begun. In this section the matter is further delineated through a treatment of his epistemological distinction between the religious sentiment and the process of rational reflection, a distinction derived from Cousin.

One need not be prejudiced, Brownson teaches, against the assertion of an immediate inspiration because some pretenders to it have been guilty of wild extravagances. The role of the religious sentiment does not preclude rationality. Warning against fanaticism, he writes:

> The inspirations of the Almighty are given, not to supersede reason, but to aid it, to purge its vision, to increase its power, and to give to the soul an impulse, an energy, an enthusiasm, which reason cannot give; and an intuition, or an inward sentiment

of moral truth, of which reason can take no cognizance. God inspires us, but he inspires us as rational, not as irrational beings, to aid us in the work of perfecting our whole nature, not to make us foreswear the exercise of a part.[17]

Subjectivity consists of both the religious sentiment and the reason through which revelation passes and is afforded rational substantiation and expression.

Religion and morality rest less on the process of rational reflection, that is, on the understanding, than on the religious sentiment. This ought not to seem strange, says Brownson, for there are a great deal of internal phenomena for which the understanding is not responsible:

There belong to human nature, passions, emotions, sentiments, affections, of which, the understanding…can take no account, which pay no deference to its ratiocinations, and even bid defiance to its laws. The feeling which we have, when contemplating a vast and tranquil sea, distant mountains with harmonious outlines, or, when marking an act of heroism, of disinterestedness, or of generous self-sacrifice for others' welfare, rises without any dependence on the understanding.[18]

These feelings can in no wise be attributed to the understanding, as if they are experienced only after a process of logical deduction. Reasoning and reflection may later occur in such a way that the feelings are rationally justified to the self, but the understanding could not have preceded them.

The understanding is void of emotion; it cannot feel. "It is calm, cold, calculating." To regard it as the exclusive epistemological principle is to disregard all that is finally meaningful:

Bring the whole of man's nature within the laws of the understanding, and you reduce religion, morality, philosophy, to a mere system of logic; you would, in the end, pronounce every thing which does not square with dry and barren dialectics, chimerical, and every thing which interest cannot appropriate, mischievous.[19]

The understanding alone cannot disclose what is ultimate to human life.

An exclusive preoccupation with the understanding, Brownson continues, is the philosophy of sensation that reigned during the last half of the eighteenth century and remains the philosophy of Brownson's America. With an autobiographical hint, he breaks with his previous empiricism:

It is no great favorite of ours. It undoubtedly has its truth; but, taken exclusively…and pushed to its last results, it would deprive man of all but a merely mechanical life, divest the heart of all emotion, wither the affections, dry up the sentiments, and sink the human race into a frigid skepticism.[20]

The understanding must be accompanied by the revelations of the reason. Indeed, in the final analysis, the testimony of the senses requires the internal sanction of the reason. The very existence of an external world, of any objective reality whatsoever, can only be credited if corroborated by the spontaneous reason.

In matters of religion, an exclusive reliance on the understanding results in the consideration of all as outward and objective, and nothing inward and subjective: "God is placed at an infinite distance from the human soul, deprived of spirituality, or at least clothed with a materiality that prevents him from reaching men's hearts, but with the aid of the understanding." The result is that a "cumbrous machinery of a formal revelation" made to the understanding is required. This is the fallacy behind the idea of revelation as the written word. Though the written word is not to be underestimated, for it can be assented to by the understanding, it is only a record of revelations made to others. Revelation is the breathing of the spirit of God immediately into the human soul. Here one can confide in the inspirations of the Almighty.[21]

In summary, the relation of revelation to reason is a virtual equation. The reason, as the religious sentiment, is spontaneous, intuitive, and dynamically active. It is to be sharply distinguished from the rational processes of the understanding, otherwise the former errors of a cold philosophy of sensation will reoccur and the mind will be plunged into a desperate skepticism. During this period of subjectivism, Brownson is so emphatic upon the role of the religious sentiment as the spontaneous reason from which all meaning flows, that it is incorrect to say that revelation is simply communicated immediately to the religious sentiment; revelation is itself tantamount to the religious sentiment.

Revelation and Nature

Nature is not a clear concept in Brownson's thought during this period. In his frequent pronouncements against the philosophy of sensation, nature is referred to negatively, in its former empiricist meaning. Because of the rise of the physical sciences, humanity's attention has turned almost exclusively to external nature. The mind is neglected and so the inspirations of the Almighty. Clearly, nature no longer possesses the status of the primary medium of revelation.

The exception to this is a vague beatific function of nature idyllically cast as it evokes in the subject a serenity of mind conducive to a communion with divine inspirations:

> Who of us has not often, when conversing with the works of our Creator, when admiring their beauty and grandeur, their loveliness and utility, been conscious of purer feelings and holier thoughts...? When alone, in the silence of nature...when the soul looks in upon herself, and we commune with our own feelings, have we not

seemed to hear a sweet and thrilling voice…? Now that voice we seemed to hear was the voice of God…the breathing of God's spirit into the soul.[22]

This is all that remains that resembles his previous understanding of nature as a Universalist.

Nevertheless, implicit in Brownson's rejection of empiricism is a turn-about from his previous mechanistic view of nature. Nature is now implied to be the external form of reason. Continuing to borrow heavily from Constant, Brownson contends that the religious sentiment always embodies itself in some external form. In an analogous fashion, the mind actively shapes and directs nature. For example, in the case of religion, it is necessary to distinguish between the sentiment and the institution:

> The sentiment results from that craving, which we have, to place ourselves in communication with invisible powers; the institutions, the form, from that craving which we also have, to render the means of that communication, we think to have discovered, regular and permanent. The consecration, regularity, and permanence, of these means, are things, with which we cannot well dispense.[23]

Since humans are religious by nature, by a fundamental law of their being, they seek to clothe, establish, or embody the sentiment in a particular positive form, that is, in an institution:

> For we take pleasure in our own sentiments only when they are attached to the universal sentiment. We do not love to nourish an opinion which no one shares with us. We aspire, for our thoughts as well as for our conduct, to the approbation of others; and we ask an external sanction to complete our internal satisfaction. Hence the necessity of religious institutions, the reason why the sentiment is always clothed with some form.[24]

The institutions are the projections of the mind outward.

Now, institutions are not equal to nature; rather, nature is analogically implied to be the external form of the sentiment when extended beyond the individual. This implies a more organic and "pliable" view of nature. Nature is no longer understood as placing its indelible impression upon the *tabula rasa* of the mind; rather, it has become the arena for the dynamic activity of the reason, the raw material for the construction of the edifice of the mind.

A theory of history is operative here, for every form contains within it a germ of opposition to future progress. To make itself increasingly impressionable upon its adherents, the form borrows images more and more material in order to disclose the sentiment. It gradually becomes petrified and humanity grows dissatisfied with it, increasingly agitating for another form.

This theory, in its relation to Brownson's doctrine of revelation and the religious sentiment, is treated immediately below. Here, it must suffice briefly to point out that as the arena for the dynamic activity of the religious sentiment, the category of nature is largely replaced by the category of history.

Revelation and History

The emergence of a dialectical theory of the positive role of history is a significant development in Brownson's thought during this period. Previously the role of history functioned largely as exemplary of a dark age of superstition and preoccupation with inaccessible heavenly realms. Now history takes on a positive and progressive role as the inevitable progress of the human race. Humanity is progressive; the religious sentiment is itself the very spirit of progress: "From Benjamin Constant's theory...we may derive much to soften our indignation at the past, and to inspire us with hope for the future. All the great institutions of former times have been good in their day, and in their places, and have had missions essential to the progress of humanity to accomplish."[25] As the religious sentiment dynamically unfolds itself in external form, shaping and directing each period of history anew, each age is seen as possessing merit of its own and history is granted value for its own sake.

Moreover, involved in this emerging theory of history is the extension of the concept of the religious sentiment from the individual to the human race understood collectively. The dynamic unfolding of the religious sentiment becomes all-embracing. What previously had been applied primarily to the individual becomes a principle of community and society.[26]

Brownson, with Constant, contends that the religious sentiment always embodies itself in some external form, that is, in an institution. The religious sentiment is a fundamental law of human nature; humanity is not religious by accident. But this fundamental law is not to be confused with the external form that it invariably takes. Though the religious sentiment always seeks to express itself externally and thus attach itself to the universal sentiment, the external form also contains a force contrary to progress:

> But every positive form, however satisfactory it may be for the present, contains a germ of opposition to future progress. It contracts, by the very effect of its duration, a stationary character, that refuses to follow the intellect in its discoveries, and the soul in its emotions, which each day renders more pure and delicate.[27]

The external form resists change because it is forced to become increasingly material in order to make a greater impression upon its adherents.

Therefore, the religious sentiment irresistibly seeks a new external form that will express its content more adequately: "The sentiment now breaks away from that form, which...has become petrified; it asks for another form, one which will not wound it, and it ceases not its exertions till it obtains it." The new form, likewise, stands in proportion to the progress of the sentiment:

> That which we worship is always the highest worth of which we can form any conception. We always embody in our religious institutions, all our ideas of the true, the beautiful, and the good. Consequently, the object of our worship, and the religious institutions we adopt, or the form with which we clothe the religious sentiment, will always be exactly proportioned to our mental development and moral progress.[28]

The institutional form advances as the religious sentiment matures.

Each religious form or institution passes through three epochs: The first is the embodiment of the religious sentiment in a determinative institutional form, insofar as humanity comes to understand its relation to invisible powers. Having satisfied its deepest craving by giving the sentiment a determinative form, humanity turns its attention to perfecting its other faculties. This signals the beginning of the second epoch. Already the destruction of the form is inevitable, for as humanity succeeds in perfecting these other faculties, it grows increasingly aware of the disproportion between the form and the progress it has made: "A conflict commences, not only between the established religion and the understanding which it insults, but between it and the religious sentiment, which it has ceased to satisfy."[29] Hence, the third epoch occurs, namely, the annihilation of the form.

Society, then, is not created in adulthood, as capable of receiving all that is to be revealed. Humans are created progressive beings; the religious sentiment is restless, maturing and expanding as demanded or allowed by the times:

> The child is set forward by the education it receives from the father; so is society by Divine Revelation, designed to educate, not the individual merely, but the species.... Education must regard the age and capacities of its subject, at first give the most simple and easy, and gradually proceed to the more complex and difficult; so God does not communicate all truth at once, but gives it in different portions, at different times, as the wants and capacities of society demand or allow. His object in all his revelations is to prepare men for the reign of benevolence.[30]

History has now nearly advanced to maturity. The present age demonstrates powers of the mind heretofore unrivaled. "The time has now come to rear the new temple."[31] The religious sentiment is to be clothed in a new form.

In early 1836, Brownson moved to Chelsea, separated from the city of Boston proper by only the Charles River. Longing to put his ideas into practice, he found a receptive audience among both the intelligentsia and the laboring classes of Boston. Burning with a reformer's zeal, he immediately established "The Society for Christian Union and Progress," published *New*

Views of Christianity, Society, and the Church as the Society's manifesto, and became the editor of the labor-oriented *Boston Reformer*. The intent of the Society was to prepare the way for a "Church of the Future" that would represent the embodiment of the religious sentiment in a new form consistent with the maturity of the age. This was to be accomplished through the unification of Christianity and the progress of the human race through social reform.

A brief review of *New Views of Christianity, Society, and the Church* summarizes Brownson's plan and serves to illustrate his theory of history during this period. He begins by reiterating Constant's doctrine of the religious sentiment. Only the sentiment is universal, permanent and indestructible. "Religion is natural to man, and he ceases to be man the moment he ceases to be religious."[32] But the sentiment is to be distinguished from religious institutions, the latter comprising the forms that the sentiment takes as humanity advances through history. As the religious sentiment is itself the principle of progress, all forms must inevitably change. This is universal law.

Currently, Brownson continues, there is a wide disparity between the religious sentiment and its institutional form. The intellectual development characteristic of the present age finds no harmonious embodiment in religious institutions. The church is outdated and the fault is its own. This state of affairs, however, is not surprising considering that the church, even at its best, failed to comprehend Christianity as taught and represented by Jesus:

> Christianity, as it existed in the mind of Jesus, was the type of the most perfect religious institution to which the human race will, probably, ever attain. It was the point where the sentiment and the institution, the idea and the symbol, the conception and its realization appear to meet and become one. But the contemporaries of Jesus were not equal to this profound thought (5).

Even Jesus' disciples failed to comprehend him. But if the age in which Jesus appeared had understood him, it would have had no need of him. Jesus appeared with regard to the future of humanity, not merely to his contemporaries. Hence, it is perfectly understandable that the age could not fully embody his ideas in its institutions.

Rather, the early church mistakenly opted for a spiritualistic interpretation of Jesus. Brownson explains:

> Spiritualism regards purity or holiness as predicable of spirit alone, and matter as essentially impure, possessing and capable of receiving nothing of the holy,—the prison house of the soul, its only hindrance to a union with God, or absorption into his essence, the cause of all uncleanliness, sin, and evil, consequently to be condemned, degraded, and as far as possible annihilated (8).

Materialism, on the other hand, entirely disregards the spiritual and heavenly in favor of counting the body and earthly everything. These two alternatives represented the warring systems of the age.

The opposition between spiritualism and materialism presupposes an original and necessary antithesis between spirit and matter, an antithesis harmonized or unified in Jesus. This harmonization represents the meaning of Jesus' claim "I and the Father are one," and is the great message of Christianity:

> Christianity declares as its great doctrine that there is no essential, no original antithesis between God and man; that neither spirit nor matter is unholy in its nature; that all things, spirit, matter, God, man, soul, body, heaven, earth, time, eternity, with all their duties and interests, are in themselves holy (10).

But the early church failed to comprehend this. Predicating only the holiness of spirit, it took its stand with spiritualism. Among the results were a denial of the humanity of Jesus, thereby inviting gnosticism; an identification of humanity's materiality with an inherent depravity, that is, with original sin; the non-materiality of Jesus' resurrection body; an erroneous doctrine of justification by imputation, for humanity could not be made holy in the material world, only in a world to come; the infallibility of the church as identified with the spiritual order and its concomitant supremacy over the civil order; and a subjugation of reason, which is human and material, to faith, which concerns the spiritual:

> Reason too is human; then it is material; to set it up against faith were to set up the material against the spiritual; the human against the divine; man against God: for the church being God by proxy, by representation, it has of course the right to consider whatever is set up against the faith it enjoins as set up against God (13).

In spite of the occasional rebellions of materialism, specifically in the forms of Arianism and Pelagianism, spiritualism was thus to remain in the ascendancy for centuries.

However, an insurrection of materialism was historically inevitable, for temporal interests and the power of human reason could not be denied. This, in essence, is the character of Protestantism and the motivating factor behind the Reformation:

> Spiritualism had exhausted its energies; it had done all it could for humanity; the time had come for the material element of our nature, which spiritualism had neglected and grossly abused, to rise from its depressed condition and contribute its share to the general progress of mankind (17).

Closely identifying the Reformation with the Renaissance, Brownson contends that Protestantism represents the reemergence of the powers of human reason in reaction to the authoritarian spiritualism of the Roman Catholic Church. Claiming the right of individuals to interpret the Bible for themselves according to the dictates of reason, the Reformation spawned a new era of philosophy "built on the absolute freedom and independence of the individual reason" (20). This modification of the previously unquestioned authority of the church introduced movement and progress into history unrivaled in past ages.

Nevertheless, the exclusively materialistic nature of Protestantism signaled its own demise. Overlooking the spiritual, Protestantism ends in philosophical materialism, that is, in a crass empiricism:

> There is full confidence in reason.[33] The method of philosophizing is the experimental. But as the point of view is the outward—matter—spirit is overlooked; matter alone admitted. Hence philosophical materialism. And philosophical materialism, in germ or developed, had been commensurate with Protestantism. When the mind becomes fixed on the external world, inasmuch as we become acquainted with that world only by means of our senses, we naturally conclude that our senses are our only source of knowledge. Hence sensism…. And from the hypothesis that our senses are our only inlets of knowledge, we are compelled to admit that nothing can be known which is not cognizable by some one or all of them. Our senses take cognizance only of matter; then we can know nothing but matter (21).

Once again, the opposition of spirit and matter asserts itself.

The influence of the philosophical materialism of Protestantism upon society at large resulted in the excesses of the French Revolution. Strictly speaking, Brownson argues, Protestantism expired in the French Revolution and since then there has been a reaction in favor of a mystical spiritualism. Once again despairing of the earth, humanity has sought refuge in heaven.[34]

Such a state of affairs, Brownson continues, conducts itself to the mission of the present age. Humanity cannot dispense with all religious institutions, for humanity must embody and express the religious sentiment. It cannot return to spiritualism, for the world and the mind are too far advanced. A return to materialism is likewise impossible, for materialism contains its own germ of destruction. Rather, a new church, a new institutional embodiment of the religious sentiment is called for: "We are to reconcile spirit and matter; that is, we must realize the atonement" (32). The Church of the Future will realize the mission of Jesus by finding divinity in humanity and humanity in divinity.

The age is equipped for such a task. Having escaped the cold formalism of philosophical materialism, humanity is once again inspired and open to the spiritual. The inspiration of the age and the maturity of the mind have demonstrated that what is found in nature and humanity is also found in

God. Betraying his continuing reliance on Channing, Brownson argues for a likeness of nature in humanity and divinity:

> This declaration gives us the hidden sense of the symbol of the God-Man. By asserting the divinity of humanity, it teaches us that we should not view that symbol as the symbol of two natures in one person, but of kindred natures in two persons. The God-Man indicates not the antithesis of God and man; nor does it stand for a being alone of its kind; but it indicates the homogeneousness of the human and divine natures, and shows that they can dwell together in love and peace. The Son of Man and the Son of God are not two persons but one—a mystery which becomes clear the very moment that the human nature is discovered to have a sameness with the divine (46).

History stands poised to enter an age of unprecedented benevolence, an age of union and progress never before experienced in the history of the race. The religious sentiment will take on an institutional form that will unify all of Christianity and reform society of the ills that have plagued it. History is progressive; the Church of the Future will come forth as a dialectical synthesis of its predecessors.

Revelation and Scripture

Scripture continues to be a rather unimportant category for Brownson during this period of his development. Its occasional mention is usually found within a polemical context. For example, he writes:

> Revelation instead of being the inspiration of God, is supposed to be the written word, and is so treated, that one can hardly help inferring that it is believed that heaven or hell depends upon "a various reading," or the rendering of a Greek particle…. We do grieve over this want of spirituality, over this materializing of the Gospel, and this converting the inspirations of the Almighty into cold doctrines and formal precepts that can be written on paper. For ourselves, we should as soon think of seizing the winged lightening and of writing it out with pen and ink as of recording the inspirations of God in a book. Men have spoken, men may speak, as they were, and are, moved by them, but what they speak is something very different from the inspirations themselves.[35]

Revelation is not Scripture, but the inspirations of God made to the soul. It is a mistake to equate the outward external expression of an inspiration with that inspiration itself: "The Bible is not revelation, but a record of the views which wise and good men, the prophets and the saints of the Jewish nation, took of it. The question, the only question, so far as the Bible is concerned, is, are those views the true views of God's revelation?"[36] The inspirations of God cannot be written down. Individuals may speak as moved by them, but what is spoken is not the inspirations themselves: "We cannot be content with the cold voice of an ancient book, or with the erring voice of mortal men, where our fathers had the living and true voice of God. We would hear God speak."[37] This can be accomplished only through listening to the voice of God within the soul:

> We must enter into ourselves, go into our own hearts. There, if we will but wait in silence, in the quietude of the soul, with the world shut out, we shall meet him, as sensibly, and hold as sweet, as instructing, and as invigorating communings with him, as did the "holy men of old, who spake as they were moved" by his spirit.[38]

Since Scripture is only a record of revelation made to others, it can only be assented to by the understanding. Scripture is like an external form, empirical and variable. In no wise can it attain the status of the religious sentiment, which can never be fully expressed in any form.

Revelation and Jesus

The role of Jesus as the God-Man, as the representative of the union and harmony of divinity and humanity, is intimately related to the emergence of Brownson's theory of the positive role of history. Jesus represents the atonement, that is, the harmonization of the divine and human that all history strives toward. He remains a medium of revelation, not so much as a communicator of objective truths, but as a symbolic representation of the ideal embodiment of the religious sentiment. The emphasis has shifted from Jesus' teachings to his person.

However, Brownson does not claim that it is Jesus who accomplishes the atonement in history. Rather, Jesus is the symbolic representation of an atonement yet to come, something Brownson at times calls the "second coming" of Jesus. Christianity existed in the mind of Christ as the perfect institutionalization of the religious sentiment in its revelatory fullness. He is the harbinger of progress and reform:

> But we would to God that all, and especially every clergyman, felt that the gospel was given to effect a great moral and social reform in man's earthly condition, that Jesus was a reformer, that the apostles were reformers, that he and they suffered martyrdom as reformers, and that whoever would be a true disciple of Jesus must love all men, even the most abandoned.... It should sink deep into our hearts, and forbid us to desist from an earnest inquiry after a remedy for all social evils of whatever name or magnitude.[39]

Jesus represented, exemplified, and personified "the realization of the idea of the right, the moral sense clothed with a practical form."[40] This realization is the all-comprehensive law of morality, namely, the love of neighbor.

The morality of the gospel constitutes its originality and peculiar feature. Jesus did not teach a new system of theological dogmas or objective truths, but embodied a purer and higher principle of morality:

> In making this assertion, we do not plunge into the arena of theological warfare, we touch not the field from which ascend the battle-shouts of conflicting sectarians; we rise to higher and broader ground, and plant our footsteps, not on the dogmas of the Gospel, but on its simple, sublime, and universal morality. We leave the dogmas about which theologians wrangle; they have their truth, have had their use, but they do not constitute the peculiarity of the Gospel.[41]

The so-called great theological truths were all known well before the time of Jesus. For example, the doctrine of the unity of God, his paternity, justice and mercy, a future state and righteous retribution were all held centuries prior to Jesus and held by many different religions and cultures:

> How men came to the knowledge of these doctrines, whether naturally or super-naturally, by a deduction of reasoning, by the unfolding of a law of their own nature, or by a direct communication from God himself, we do not now inquire. It is sufficient...that they were known before the coming of Christ.... It is important that we do not forget this. We believe in the originality of the Gospel; but if the Gospel be asserted to be the revelation of a mere system of theology, its originality remains to be proved. Its originality, and its only peculiarity...is in its morality.[42]

Hence, the gospel does not equal the revelation of a system of theology or set of objective truths, but is constituted by Jesus' representation and embodiment of the moral sentiment of love.

However, Jesus' representation and embodiment of the moral sentiment is not merely exemplary. He plays a providential role as a historical figure of decisive influence who advances history through the revelatory fullness of his religious sentiment. Though still undeveloped, it is on this point that the intimate relationship of the role of history and the role of Jesus begins to emerge in Brownson's thought in the form of the concept of "providential men," which he derives from the Saint-Simonians. Providential men were people regarded as individuals extraordinary to their times who, by virtue of superior God-given insight, decisively moved history forward toward greater progress and reform.

Though it does not play a decisive role in Brownson's thought during this period, the concept of providential men begins to emerge, especially, though not exclusively, in regard to Jesus. During this period Brownson consistently identifies the alleged superior insight of providential men with his doctrine of the religious sentiment as naturally progressive. It may be safely concluded, therefore, that a providential man would embody and teach a progressive revelation. Brownson even hoped such an individual would soon emerge in America.[43]

Transition: From Pure to Imperfect Transcendentalism

Brownson's thought during this period was, in large part, a reaction to his experience as a Universalist. The barrenness of his previous empiricism gives way to the lively doctrine of the religious sentiment, which in turn gives rise to a strong subjectivism. As late as July, 1836, he writes:

> Religion is the upleaping of the soul towards the infinite; it is a love, a worship of spirit, or spirit in man, in the universe, and he only is the successful teacher of religion who can unfold the spiritual nature, and show to the mind the infinite, the God, in each individual, to be loved, venerated and adored.[44]

His period of subjectivism is brief, but intense. It would have a formative influence on his subsequent thought.

By September of that year there are indications of a transitional movement beyond subjectivism to an attempted synthesis or harmonization of subject and object. Brownson's intellectual identity begins, in the terminology of Octavius Brook Frothingham, to shift from a "pure" Transcendentalism into an "imperfect" Transcendentalism.[45] Carey explains:

> The "pure" Transcendentalists were those who believed that human beings were already in possession of all supernatural truths. The "imperfects" were those who saw transcendental philosophy as a means for confirming their faith in supernatural realities; they held that human beings had only the capacity for receiving (not possessing) supernatural realities by means of a divine revelation.

Emerson is typical of the "pure," Brownson the "imperfect":

> With respect to religion…there were those like Emerson who emphasized intuition and "reason" to such an extent that they see no need of external revelation and historic Christianity; and those like Brownson who emphasized intuition and "Spontaneous Reason" as a primitive revelation or universal inspiration that provided the *a priori* conditions for the reception of revelation.[46]

Indeed, Brownson's reaction to the publication of Emerson's *Nature* (1836) is one of two significant factors that leads Brownson away from the subjectivism of "pure" Transcendentalism. Similarly, Brownson continues to affirm the role of religion in social progress, not merely through the moral improvement of the individual, as the "pure" Transcendentalists tend to argue, but as the expression of a communal and institutional embodiment of the religious sentiment, leading directly to the improvement of society.[47] Brownson's own "Society for Christian Union and Progress," stands as an example.

The other significant influence is French Eclecticism, in particular the work of Cousin. It is Cousin's impact upon Brownson that signals the next stage of his intellectual development. As such, it is treated in the following chapter. Brownson's review of *Nature*, however, displays his growing uneasiness with the subjectivism that also characterizes his own thought. In effect, he recognizes in Emerson the logical conclusion of the principles of his own thought and begins the movement toward a more balanced orientation.

After praising the work for its beauty and power, and welcoming it as "proof that the mind is about to receive a new and more glorious manifestation," Brownson proceeds to point out what he regards as a weighty philosophical problem:

> He seems seriously to doubt the existence of the external world except as an [sic] picture which God stamps on the mind. He all but worships what his senses seem to present him, and yet is not certain that all that which his senses place out of him, is not after all the mere subjective laws of his own being, existing only to the eye.[48]

Brownson appreciates Emerson's subordination of nature to spirit and understanding to reason, but distinguishes himself from Emerson's tendencies toward idealism and an underestimation of the understanding:

> The Reason is undoubtedly our only light, our only criterion of certainty; but we think the Reason vouches for the truth of the senses as decidedly and as immediately as it does for its own conceptions. He who denies the testimony of his senses, seems to us to have no ground for believing the apperception of consciousness; and to deny those is to set oneself afloat upon the ocean of universal scepticism.[49]

To speak of the external world as phenomenal, as appearance, does not entail questioning its existence. Moreover, Emerson's position entails pantheism:

> Man is phenomenal in the same sense as is the universe, but man exists. The author calls him "the apparition of God." The apparition exists as certainly as God exists, though it exists as an apparition, not as absolute being. God is absolute being. Whatever is absolute is God; but God is not the universe, God is not man; man and the universe exist as manifestations of God. His existence is absolute, theirs is relative, but real.[50]

Thus Brownson begins to move away from subjectivism in order to entertain the philosophical questions that would occupy his mind and recast his conception of revelation. Indeed, the dynamics of the problems that emerge would shape his thought decisively, not only in the years prior to his conversion to Roman Catholicism, but for the rest of his life.

CHAPTER THREE

The Attempted Synthesis (1836–1841)

THE DEPENDENCE OF revelation on empirical evidence that had character-ized the first period of Brownson's career gave way, under various influences, to a virtual coalescence of revelation with the intuiting subject during the second. The third period, addressed in this chapter, consists of Brownson's attempt to forge a synthesis of the two extremes through the adaptation of Cousin's eclectic philosophical system—so called for its attempt to draw upon the leading principles of major philosophical schools and to form them into a coherent whole, containing elements of all, but resulting in a system unlike any.

Brownson had been reading Cousin since 1833 and in addition to aiding in the development of his thought, the gradual adaptation of Cousin's sys-tem supplied Brownson with the systematic means for analyzing the philoso-phical and theological systems prevalent at the time.[1] But its chief value consisted in its ability to supply, through a painstaking method of observa-tion and induction, a philosophy designed to explain and verify revealed re-ligion, which had lost its hold upon the understanding. For this reason, Brownson's advocacy of Cousin's eclectic philosophy is quite unabashed dur-ing most of this period, for insofar as its attempt to verify revealed religion is successful, Christian belief is justified. To his mentor he wrote:

> Your work, Sir, found me sunk in a vague sentimentalism, no longer a sceptic, but unable to find any scientific basis for my belief. I despaired of passing from the sub-jective to the objective. You have corrected & aided me; you have enabled me to find a scientific basis for my belief in Nature, in God and Immortality, and I thank you again and again for the service you have done me.[2]

Cousin's influence upon Brownson's thought was large and lasting.

It is also true that while Brownson supplies little modification of Cousin's system, one does detect occasional hesitancy in his adaptation. A certain uneasiness shows from time to time, especially with respect to the further development of his christology in reaction to the perceived radical articulations of the "pure" Transcendentalists, Emerson in particular, though later Parker. Though of some initial aid, Cousin's system fails to supply Brownson with the necessary means of accomplishing the desired development.

These were tumultuous years for the nation, marked by the economic panic of 1837 and the presidential election of 1840, events that spurs Brownson to greater social analysis and critique of the American economic system.[3] Brownson remains a social radical and his highly controversial article "The Laboring Classes,"[4] a quasi-Marxist indictment of American social, political, and economic orders, may have helped lead to the defeat of Martin Van Buren. The election certainly sours Brownson on the political process and is responsible, in part, for a significant amount of intellectual dissonance. But as always, Brownson seeks religious and philosophical clarity, not solely for the sake of intellectual clarity, but for the sake of social progress.

Another important event in Brownson's development occurs in 1838 with the establishment of the *Boston Quarterly Review*, with Brownson as its editor and main contributor. Free of editorial interference, Brownson once again possesses a forum for the expression and propagation of his ideas. Called "the most philosophical of all the periodicals connected with the movement,"[5] the journal meticulously scrutinizes both the Transcendentalists and their opponents.

Noteworthy also is Brownson's reading of Jonathan Edwards (1703–1758) during this period, which initiates a significant shift in his christology and a gradual reemergence of his childhood orthodoxy.[6] Edward's *History of the Work of Redemption* (1739) was widely read during the early nineteenth century. Brownson had read it early in life and again in the late 1830s, when he tends to read Edwards as a type of "proto-Romantic." Brownson is clearly impressed with Edward's emphasis upon a spiritual and inward light of inspiration. Edward's revolutionary development of a post-millennialist eschatology within the socio-political context of the "First Great Awakening" of the 1740s also appeals to Brownson for its inclusion of the principle of progress within history. Though the influence of Edwards is not clearly recognizable, by July of 1839 Brownson could write: "Were we obliged to be either a Unitarian or a Calvinist, with our present views, we should unhesitatingly prefer to be a Calvinist."[7] Though perhaps intended solely for his Unitarian opponents, such seemingly out of place statements should not be underestimated.

Finally one should also be aware that Brownson begins to read Leroux during this period. Leroux's influence would refine Brownson's attempted synthesis in the years prior to his conversion to Roman Catholicism and is addressed in the following chapter. Nevertheless, it must be emphasized that little significant wavering from his allegiance to Cousin occurs until 1842.

This chapter consists almost entirely of an exposition of Brownson's interpretation and adaptation of Cousin's thought. After introductory sections, the now familiar categories relating revelation to reason, nature, history, Scripture, and Jesus, continue to be employed.

Brownson and the Transcendentalists

By 1836 Brownson was actively participating in the flurry of Boston intellectual life. These were tumultuous years for Brownson and his cohorts, marked by the growing controversy between the post-Kantian idealism of the Transcendentalists and the Lockean empiricism of the conservative Unitarians. The "pure" Transcendentalists, moreover, were more philosophically akin to Coleridge and German Idealism than Brownson could now allow. Brownson exhibits the influx of French Romantic and eclectic themes, a more "imperfect" form of Transcendentalism, not well tolerated by the likes of Emerson and Parker. Though Brownson was a "charter member" of the Transcendentalist Club,[8] his eclecticism, as well as his tendency to alienate the genteel Boston intellectuals with his volatile personality, results in his place at the periphery of the movement and his drift away from Transcendentalism.[9]

An involved study of the varying phenomena and diverse individuals who comprise the Transcendentalist movement would be inappropriate and unnecessary for a study such as this. However, it is important to circumscribe the movement briefly, given Brownson's involvement with it. His perception of his relation to the Transcendentalists, as revealed in his writings, betrays the movement of his own thought toward an eclectic approach and an attempt at synthesis.

Drawing chiefly upon Romantic and Idealist impulses imported to America in the late 1820s and early 1830s, Transcendentalism represents a reaction to the Lockean empiricism of a Unitarianism shaped largely by Enlightenment rationality. Though the origins of Unitarianism are found in the rationalist reaction to the "Great Awakening" of the previous century, the movement always possessed a type of liberal piety that served to soften its tendency toward rather cold and abstract pronouncements.[10] Now these influences combined and gave rise to a full-fledged philosophical and theological reaction to the reigning empiricism. Emerson's "Divinity School Address" blew the lid off the controversy in 1838 and established him as the main spokesman for the "new views." The defense of conservative Unitarianism fell to Andrews Norton (1786–1853), a biblical scholar and Harvard professor.[11]

The controversy between the Unitarian rationalists and the Transcendentalists often centered around the question of miracles. Norton, for example, attempted to defend the truth of Christianity by demonstrating and proving the reality and supernatural character of miracles. To his Enlightenment mind, the reality of the supernatural implied the suspension or violation of the laws of nature. According to his deistical view of God and mechanistic view of the universe, God is active in nature only through intervention from the outside. If the miraculous claims of Christianity can be demonstrated as suspensions of the laws of nature, then external evidence is gained in support of the existence of God and his revelation to humanity. Consequently, the act of belief tends to be reduced to assent or acknowledgement in the face of evidence. Christianity is deemed correct and thus worthy of belief.

The Transcendentalists, on the other hand, were less inclined to regard the role of miracles as proof on the supernatural. Their Romantic minds required no such proof, for the supernatural is regarded as at work in all things natural, giving all a miraculous character. Nature, far from being in need of divine intervention, is regarded as constantly expressing the divine presence. And one need only look within the self for evidence of the divine, even the divine itself. The revelation and activity of God is also found within the self and is found immediately. Since revelation is immediately intuited by the mind or soul, the mediating role of miracles in de-emphasized.

Brownson regards arguments that present miracles as the proof of the reality and claims of revelation as guilty of committing the same error of confusing revelation with arguments offered to profer its existence and legitimate its authority. In order to know a miracle to be from God, argues Brownson, a prior belief in God is required:

> Before a miracle can be admitted to be from God, it must be known there is a God; and before it can be alleged as a proof of one God, it must be known with *infallible certainty*, that there is only one God who can perform it. So then, before the miracle can authenticate a revelation of the one God, it must be known that there is but one God; all that the miracle is designed to prove must, then, be believed before the miracle can prove anything.[12]

Brownson's position is closer to that of the Transcendentalists, yet he posits an objectivity to the existence of God that reaches beyond Transcendentalism and anticipates his more eclectic approach.

For the purpose of this study it is crucial to focus upon Brownson's perception of the epistemological presuppositions of Transcendentalism and his role in the controversy. Though the members of the movement differ considerably in their opinions concerning a broad range of issues, Brownson recognizes that they are united in their adherence and loyalty to the belief in the ability of the mind to intuit immediately the realities of the spiritual world. Likewise, they are equally opposed to any reduction and confinement of knowledge and certainty to the senses. Including himself among them, Brownson writes:

> They differ widely in their opinions, and agree in little except in their common opposition to the old school. They do not swear by Locke, and they recognize no authority in matters of opinion but the human mind, whether termed the reason with some of them, or the soul with others....No single term can describe them. Nothing can be more unjust to them, or more likely to mislead the public than to lump them all together, and predicate the same things of all of them.[13]

Their "common opposition to the old school," however, is rooted in a deeper concern: "The real aim of the Transcendentalists is to ascertain a solid ground for faith in the reality of the spiritual world. Their speculations have reference in the main to the grounds of human knowledge. Can we know anything? If so, how and what?"[14] This essentially religious concern cannot be answered adequately by the advocates of empiricism. The system of philosophy of which Locke is the greatest modern representative and to which Norton clearly adheres, does not recognize the power of the mind to transcend the senses. Religion, therefore, is reduced to the production of evidences for the existence of spiritual realities, for it cannot know them directly:

> [The Transcendentalists] have therefore looked into the consciousness, examined human nature anew, to see if they could not find in man the power of recognizing and of knowing objects which transcend the reach of the senses. This power they profess to have discovered. They claim for man the power, not of discovering, but of knowing by intuition the spiritual world. According to them objects of religious faith are not merely objects believed on testimony, but objects of science, of which we may have a true inward experience of which we may have a direct and immediate knowledge.[15]

This is the crux of the matter, Brownson argues. If, finally, there can be no intuition, no direct and immediate perception of the realities to which Christianity lays claim, humanity is ultimately cast into universal skepticism.

The Influence of Victor Cousin

This is not all Brownson has to say concerning the Transcendentalists. When writing for the general public he tends to identify himself with them, enlisting his literary talents in support of their cause. But within their own circles, and under Cousin's influence, Brownson turns considerably more critical:

> So far as Transcendentalism is understood to be the recognition in man of the capacity of knowing truth intuitively, or of attaining to a scientific knowledge of an order of existence transcending the reach of the senses, and of which we have no sensible experience, we are Transcendentalists. But when it is understood to mean, that feeling is to be placed above reason, dreaming above reflection, and instinctive intimation above scientific exposition, we must disown it, and deny that we are Transcendentalists.[16]

The difficulties Brownson detected in "Nature" continue to plague Emerson's "Divinity School Address."[17] Emerson, says Brownson, mutilates the mind by ignoring the process of reflection, that is, the understanding. Exclusive reliance upon the reason leads to irrationalism and a false sentimentalism.

Brownson continues, rather, to insist upon Cousin's distinction between the reason and understanding, the distinction becoming the critical apparatus of Brownson's critique of the Transcendentalists. Demanding more mental precision, he strives for balance: "In running away from the sensualism of Locke, I would take care not to lose sight of that portion of reality which his system embraced; and in rejecting logic as an originator of ideas, I would still hold fast to it, as an essential instrument for clearing up our ideas, arranging them in their systematic order, and enabling us to master them."[18] The eclecticism of Cousin is to be preferred to the tendency of the Transcendentalists to ignore the understanding and fall into a vague sentimentalism. Precision and balance is called for; a synthetic approach must reconcile the polarities. "We are religious only at the expense of our logic," accused Brownson. If religion is to be sustained as anything more than a vague, intangible sentiment, it must be sustained by philosophy.[19]

But the reigning philosophy of Lockean empiricism has eclipsed religion from the realm of common sense by tracing all the facts of consciousness back to the senses.[20] Far from confirming through its explanations and reflections the universal beliefs and experiences of humanity, it contradicts them, destroying certitude in its wake. All that remains is the understanding, devoid of its object and turned upon itself.

Brownson had identified this problem previously and in reaction had advocated Constant's theme of the religious sentiment and strongly endorsed the Transcendentalists. Through Cousin, however, Brownson regains the importance of the understanding as supplying rational confirmation and articulation of the revelations of the religious sentiment. Through the reflection of the understanding, philosophical justification could be issued in support of the claims of common sense.

Through Cousin, the distinction Brownson had drawn between the religious sentiment and the understanding (between the spontaneous reason and the mental process of reflection) becomes increasingly referred to as the difference between the impersonal reason and the personal reason. The impersonal reason embraces all that was claimed with respect to the religious sentiment, but with an emphasis upon its identification with the Absolute, or God. It reveals that which cannot be derived from external nature, nor willed by the self:

> The reason, though appearing in us, is not our *self*. It is independent of us, and in no sense subject to our personality. If it depended on our personality, or if it constituted our personality, we could control its conceptions, prescribe its laws, and compel it to speak according to our pleasure. Its conceptions would be ours, as much and in the same sense, as our intentions; its revelations, would be our revelations, that is, revelations of ourselves, and its truths would be our truths.[21]

The impersonal reason corresponds to the common sense of humanity and to its religious beliefs, for all know and desire to believe that neither God nor the external world is a mere projection of the self: "Who is prepared to admit such a conclusion?…Who does not feel, who does not know, that the truth is not his,—is nobody's, but independent of everybody." If the reason is not impersonal, it can reveal no existences outside the self, nor provide for anything other than a subjective authority. Skepticism would result, for there could be no justification for belief in that which lies beyond the self. In "Cousin's Philosophy," Brownson writes:

> To deprive the reason of all but a subjective authority, to allow it no validity out of the sphere of our own personality, is to deprive it of all legitimate authority, and to place philosophy on the route to a new and original skepticism. If the reason have no authority out of the sphere of the personality…it can reveal to us no existences which lie beyond ourselves. Such may be the laws of our nature, that we cannot help believing that we are, that there is an external world, and God; but our belief can repose on no scientific basis. There is nothing to assure us, that it is not a mere illusion.[22]

Failure to admit the impersonality of the reason is tantamount to admitting the unknowability of God. But to admit the impersonality of the reason is to allow it to become the legitimate authority for all it reveals. No longer confined to subjectivity, it conducts of itself to an equally legitimate ontology.

Revelation and Reason

It is through the impersonal, spontaneous reason that the spiritual world is revealed and known. The reason is intuitive, providing direct and immediate knowledge of that which transcends the senses. By means of Cousin's philosophy, Brownson provides this presupposition with philosophical elaboration and an intellectual sophistication that his previous thought had lacked. The resulting epistemology begins to harmonize the previous disparities of his thought and enables him to assert more confidently the grounds of faith in the claims of Christianity.

Following Cousin, Brownson admits that careful observation reveals "a class or order of phenomena in the consciousness," resulting from the impression of sensation upon the human mind. This class of phenomena derived from the external world corresponds to the mental faculty properly termed the "sensibility." However, careful observation also reveals two other classes of phenomena corresponding to the mental faculties termed the "activity" and the "reason." The internal phenomena that the mind itself produces or wills belong to the activity; to the reason belong all purely internal and intellectual facts that the mind itself is conscious of not having produced and which cannot be derived through the sensation of external nature. These three faculties are essentially distinct, though never found in isolation from each other. They exist in every fact of consciousness (41–3).

The reason, therefore, is distinguished from the sensibility, for its phenomena are not derived from external nature. It is also distinguished from the activity, for it is not willed or caused by the mind itself. It extends to the objective as well as the subjective, to beings as well as phenomena, to a knowledge of the external world and God as well as the self. Moreover, it does so immediately, in every fact of consciousness. Brownson demonstrates his assertion as follows.

Every fact of consciousness involves a voluntary act of attention (or will, activity) that is characterized by a consideration of the self as its cause. This cause is simply individuality or personality, what is called the "I" or "me," which cannot be doubted nor confounded with another:

> We find *ourselves* then, in the fact of consciousness, and we find ourselves as cause, a creative force. This is the radical idea we have of ourselves. We know ourselves under no other character than that of a cause, and we exist for ourselves no farther than we are a cause. The bounds of our causality are the bounds of our existence (47).

Every fact of consciousness involves a conception of the self as cause.

The senses are continually bombarded with impressions from outside the self. These impressions do not come to consciousness other than through the intervention of attention, that is, the consciousness of sensation begins through an act of attention. As every fact of consciousness involves an act of attention characterized by the self as cause, so it is that the self is the cause of attending to impressions made upon the organs of sense.

Though the self is the cause of attending to impressions, it does not follow that the self is the cause of the impressions. "We receive sensations, we do not cause them." They must be referred to a cause outside the self. This cause is as certain as the cause involved in the act of attention: "The existence of this exterior cause is as certain to us as our own existence; for the phenomenon,—sensation,—which suggests it, is as certain to us, as the phenomenon,—act of attention,—which suggests to us our existence. Both too, are given together, in the same phenomenon" (47–8). Every fact of consciousness includes a conception of the self, of one's existence, and a conception of that which is not the self, namely, external nature.

Likewise, there is a meeting of the two causes, one located in the act of attention originating in the self, and one located in sensation originating in external nature. These two causes necessarily limit each other; one cannot be conceived without the other and to conceive of them at all is to distinguish them in the mind as relative and finite:

> The cause, which we are, meets resistance…in that variety of causes…of which we are conscious, which we do not produce and which are purely affective and involuntary; and these causes themselves are limited and bounded by that voluntary cause which we are. We resist them as they resist us, and, to a certain extent, limit their action as they limit ours. It is only in the meeting, the clashing of the two causes, it is only in their conflict, that either is revealed to us (47–8).

The relativity and finitude of the two causes, attention and sensation, is revealed in their clashing and limiting action upon each other.

But if the two causes are present in the consciousness as finite and relative, they must exist there only as contrasted with a conception of the infinite and absolute. Consequently, in every fact of consciousness is found a conception of the self and the non-self, of personality and of external nature, existing as finite and relative causes; and a conception of the infinite and absolute with which the finite and relative must be contrasted in order to be conceived. It is the reason which perceives the limiting action and relativity of the two finite causes, as well as their contrasting relation to the infinite, "the cause of all Causes":

> The internal and personal cause which we are, and the exterior causes which we call nature, are undeniably causes in relation to their own causes, giving them as relative and limited causes, prevents us from stopping with them as causes which are sufficient for themselves, and forces us to refer them to a supreme Cause (49).

Finally, then, in every fact of consciousness is found a conception of the existence of the self, the existence of the external world, and the existence of the infinite cause, God.

Hence, God exists in relation to humanity as cause. This is not, however, an inference of the absolute from the relative, the infinite from the finite, God from the self and the non-self. Such an inference leads to atheism, pantheism or egoism. Atheism, Brownson argues, would result from such exclusive contemplation of the phenomena of sensibility. The consequences of this preoccupation is a denial of the infinite, a confusion of the idea of unity with that of mere totality. The atheist cannot perceive of a cause that produces the diversity and multiplicity of the universe around him; he sinks God into nature. The reversal of atheism in pantheism. It originates in the exclusive contemplation of the phenomena of the reason, a preoccupation with the infinite. The pantheist fails to note things in their diversity and multiplicity, asserting the absolute unity and identity of all that is. While atheism sees no God, pantheism sees nothing but God. It sinks nature into God. Egoism stems from a preoccupation with the phenomena of the activity, or will. The activity possesses a real creative power, as evidenced by the portion of consciousness that consists of facts of one's own creating. Since the activity is involved in every act of intelligence, and is indeed the proper personality, knowledge is predicated of the self. But if the activity, which is subjective, is taken exclusively, nothing can be posited. Pure subjectivism results, for both God and nature are sunk into the self.[23]

As philosophy exists in order to explain and verify religion, so the reflective process of the understanding, the subjective and personal side of the reason, does not originate or determine the content of the spontaneous impersonal reason, but verifies and explains it. Both the infinite and the finite are given together as primitive data, as the necessary condition for the very process of reasoning:

> The Absolute is no logical creation, no production of reasoning. It could not be deduced from the relative. No dialectic skill has ever yet been able to draw the infinite from the finite, the unconditioned from the conditioned. Both terms are given together, both are primitive *data*, without which no reasoning could possibly take place (50).

Remove the idea of either the infinite or the finite and any single intellectual act would be impossible. One cannot be conceived without the other.

Furthermore, the ideas of the infinite and the finite do not merely coexist, they are related to each other as cause and effect. The infinite is absolute cause of all finitude. Consequently, the impersonal reason reveals the infinite, the finite, and their relation. All three comprise the primitive data of the intellect and the starting point of all reasoning. All three are present before the understanding begins to act. "All three...are developed simultaneously in the first fact of the intellectual life." Existing as the necessary conditions of all reasoning, they reveal to us God, the external world, and ourselves:

> Our belief in God, in nature, in our own existence, is the result of no reasoning. When we first turned our minds inward in the act of reflection, we found that be-

lief. We had it, and every man has it, from the dawn of the intellect. It does not proceed then from reflection; and, as reflection is the only intellectual act in which we have any agency, it follows that it does not exist in consequence of any thing we have willed or done. It is prior to *our* action, and independent of it....It must be a primitive, spontaneous belief, the result of the spontaneity of the reason (51).

The spontaneous reason, as impersonal and objective, is a legitimate authority for that which it reveals. Its credibility, upon which all these claims depend, need not nor cannot be proven. The spontaneous reason is self-evident; as such, it is the least susceptible to proof. Nevertheless, we may be as sure of the existence of God and the external world as we are sure of our own existence, which likewise cannot be proven. No higher authority is needed, no greater degree of certainty desired.

In summary, an analysis of the consciousness of the individual reduces all phenomena to three ideas: that of the infinite, the finite, and their relation. These are the primitive elements of the intelligence, discernible by, but not originating in, the understanding. Their spontaneous development is owing not to the reflective powers of human philosophizing, but to God:

They are, then, connate, inherent, underived....The development of the idea of the infinite in the understanding, is not attained by human agency. It is effected by the spontaneous working of the reason. The spontaneous development of the idea of the infinite, in the human intelligence, is precisely what the human race means, and always has meant, by the revelation of God.[24]

Finally, the revelations of the spontaneous reason constitute the sure ground of faith in the claims of Christianity. Cousin's system affords Brownson a temporary foundation: "His system is the only one, that has come to my knowledge, which enables me to explain, on rational principles, the phenomenon of revelation, and to find firm ground for my faith as a Christian."[25] For a time, Brownson's unrelenting pursuit of a rational basis for Christianity, the conditions for the possibility of revelation, has been fulfilled.

Revelation and Nature

The effect of Cousin's thought upon Brownson's understanding of the role of nature and its relation to revelation consists in the emergence of the theme of creation as the necessary manifestation of absolute intelligence itself. Brownson's previous identification of revelation with the religious sentiment had transformed his mechanistic view of nature to that of an arena for the dynamic activity of the mind. Under Cousin's influence, that activity of the mind becomes the manifestation of the infinite, of absolute cause, of God.

Having begun with a careful analysis of the facts of consciousness and proceeding from their identification to a notion of God as infinite Cause, Brownson now completes the process by moving from God to nature. Nature is more than the raw material for erecting the edifice of the mind, it is the necessary consequent of absolute cause. If the spontaneous reason can reveal the absolute, it must itself be absolute, for it cannot reveal that which it has not in itself. God really does appear in us, Brownson claims:

> The reason, taken absolutely, we have said is identical with God....The reason is God; it appears in us, therefore, God appears in us. The light of reason, the light by which we see and know all that we do see and know, is truly the light of God. The voice of the spontaneous reason is the voice of God; those who speak by its authority, speak by the authority of God, and what they utter is a real revelation.[26]

God is given immediately in every fact of consciousness and is given as infinite, absolute cause.

It is not enough, Brownson continues, to posit God as pure essence, as without attribute or quality. It is impossible to get at the idea of God as it exists in the common sense of humanity, that is, as creator, unless his essence is also posited as absolute cause and absolute intelligence:

> If God be pure essence, he cannot be legitimately regarded as intelligent. If he create, it must be unconsciously, without knowing either himself, or what he does. He becomes a dark, blind necessity, from which the universe is fatally evolved. He then cannot be a person, and then nothing which corresponds to our idea of God. Furthermore, if he be mere essence, mere being, without attribute or quality, he cannot create. There can be no creation, nor even an evolution of himself, for he contains nothing to be evolved. Unity multiplied by unity yields only unity.[27]

God is given not only as absolute being, but as absolute cause and absolute intelligence, or reason.

However, this assertion does not demonstrate or prove God's freedom. Far from maintaining a doctrine of *creatio ex nihilo*, Brownson's thought in this respect has developed into a form of emanationism. To posit God as absolute cause implies necessary creation, for to be a cause is necessarily to cause something. He ceases to exist to us "in exact proportion as he ceases to be creator."[28] Out of what, then, does God create? He cannot create out of already existing materials, for this would entail the eternality of two absolutes, God and matter. Nor can he create out of nothing, for nothing can be created from nothing. Rather, God creates out of himself, that is, out of absolute intelligence, or reason. The universe manifests the absolute intelligence of its Creator:

> God can manifest only what is in himself. He is thought, intelligence itself. Consequently, there is in creation nothing but thought, intelligence. In nature, as in hu-

manity, the supreme Reason is manifested, and there, where we had fancied all was dead and without thought, we are now enabled to see all living and essentially intellectual. There is no dead matter, there are no fatal causes; nature is thought, and God is its personality.[29]

Not only humanity, but the universe itself, bears the same relation to God as intelligence as it does to God as cause. If God in his essence is both intelligence and cause, it simply follows that he must create the universe according to the laws or principles of that essence.[30]

Brownson responds to the criticism that this position represents God as necessary cause, rather than free and independent cause, by claiming the distinction to be a solecism. It is incongruous to posit necessary cause over against free cause, for a cause is a cause only insofar as it is free: "There is and can be no such thing as necessary causes, except in a relative sense. All cause in the last analysis must be free, and precisely of the nature of that cause which in ourselves we term power of willing." To conceive of God as creating under necessity is to conceive of him as a secondary cause. If God is God as we understand him to be, he is independent and free. Nevertheless, creation is necessary in the following manner:

> Being a cause he [God] must cause something, otherwise he would be merely a possible cause and not an actual cause...which would be to us as no cause at all....Now a God who actually creates must needs be conceived of in connexion with actual creation. The creation of the world follows as a necessary consequence of a acual [sic] creator without conceiving of an actual creation. In this sense creation is necessary.[31]

Moreover, unless God be conceived as the actual, not just potential, cause of creation, there is no way he can be posited in such a way as to justify the common sense of humanity. "The God of common sense is always the God who actually creates the world, who is the actual cause of the universe."[32] It is in the common sense of humanity, not in philosophical systems, that the primitive conceptions of reason are found.

It may be confidently asserted, therefore, that the universe rests on a rational basis. As the manifestation of divine intelligence, it is rationally accessible and open to analysis. Once having risen through psychological observation and induction to God as absolute reason and intelligence, the universe may be logically deduced, for its laws are *a priori* the laws of its Creator.[33]

Revelation and History

Though one finds the attention paid to the category of history somewhat diminished in comparison to Brownson's immediately preceding period, the importance of the development of Brownson's thought on this score should not be minimized. Influenced by Constant and the Saint-Simonians, Brownson previously had posited humanity as progressive and the religious sentiment as the very spirit of that progress. Moreover, the themes of progress and the religious sentiment had been applied to the human race collectively, thereby establishing the principles of community and society. Now, continuing to draw from Cousin's work, Brownson infers a doctrine of providence that consists of the integration of his emerging doctrine of creation with his already present dialectical view of the positive role of history and the inevitable progress of the human race. This would prove decisive and play a major role in his thought in the near future.

If God is providentially involved in the development of humanity, he must be involved in such a way as is consistent with his own existence: "If we admit the universal providence of God in the developments of Humanity, we must admit it under the character which is essential to God. God is free and independent, but he always acts in accordance with his own nature....When we conceive of God as acting, we must conceive of him as acting in harmony with himself."[34] As the universe bears an affinity to the intelligence that creates it, so too the providential care its Creator affords. Providence bears the same relation to the essence of God as does creation, for it is inconceivable to posit the divine creation of humanity and nature without simultaneously positing the divine care and protection under which they have been placed, and to which the common sense of all humanity testifies.[35]

It follows that humanity is the agent of God's providential care, for God has created it with a nature and mission derived from and consistent with the divine reason. Humanity is determined by its very constitution to fulfill its providential mission in history. Hence, humanity and the universe, in their character and progression, are united to God in their derivative rationality.

Accordingly, the progression of humanity in history is reducible to a science, that is, it can be known and demonstrated. The phenomena of nature and of history can be reduced to a science because their laws and principles are coincident with those of the mind. Philosophy emerged at the beginning of history when humanity inevitably began to reflect upon the three ideas that constituted the primitive mind as the divine intelligence. Since there is nothing in humanity that is not reducible to the idea of the infinite, the idea of the finite, and the idea of their relation, philosophical reflection upon humanity and its development has always contained the three ideas.[36]

However, the three ideas may be found in differing degrees of development; one or another tends to emerge as dominant. Indeed, the dominance of one idea over the others marks the different epochs of history. Likewise, various philosophical schools and orientations emerge during the different epochs (which interestingly follow the same chronology as Brownson's intellectual development.) *Sensualism* emerges when philosophical reflection is directed exclusively to the facts of the sensibility, for the facts of the reason and the activity are overlooked. The result is an exclusive concern with the finite and the reduction of all ideas to those derived from sensation. The understandable reaction is *Idealism*, which focuses only upon the facts of the reflective and personal reason. The result is a preoccupation with the mental processes and the inability to account adequately for the facts of the sensibility and the finite. Weary of the seemingly unending quarrels between the two schools, *Skepticism* arises, challenging them to re-examine the means by which they have attained their conclusion. A frequent result is the refuge of *Mysticism*, which rejects reflection and philosophy altogether and rests upon the spontaneous and impersonal reason. But this alternative denies the existence of the understanding.[37]

All of these schools, says Brownson, contain truth insofar as they concern themselves with the primitive ideas of the human mind. Yet, their tendency to reduce all phenomena to one idea leaves them inadequate. Happily, the ideas that constitute humanity cannot long be overlooked. *Eclecticism*, therefore, is the only possibility. Humanity has progressed to the ability of recognizing the truth contained in each system; no element of humanity is neglected:

> The great mission of the age is to unite the infinite and the finite. Union, harmony, whence proceed peace and love, are the points to be aimed at. We of the nineteenth century appear in the world as mediators. In philosophy, theology, government, art, industry, we are to conciliate hostile feeling, and harmonize conflicting principles and interests.[38]

That which is fundamentally true of human nature is fundamentally true of human history. This affords human history immeasurable value as the providential progression of the human mind.

The facts of consciousness, which correspond to the mental faculties identified as the reason, the sensibility, and the activity or will, in turn correspond to the facts of history as they are reducible to providence, nature and humanity. As finite and limiting causes, nature and humanity can be conceived only as contrasted with the infinite, that is, only in relation to providence. Consequently, there can be only three causes at work in history, namely, humanity, nature, and providence.

Humanity, for example, functions as a cause in history through the action of its intelligence, passion, and volition. As a product of the infinite

Reason, humanity is constituted in harmony with its laws. It follows that rational measure may be taken of humanity's actions. Nature, through the influence of such factors as climate, soil, and geographical position, also functions as a cause in history. Nature is also the product of intelligence, so natural facts are reducible to the laws of reason. Finally providence, through revelation, inspiration, and supernatural guidance, functions as cause in history. As the action and control of the eternal Reason itself, it is always in harmony with eternal Reason. Hence, providential facts also fall within the scope of the reason and are reducible to its laws.[39]

The importance of this development in Brownson's thought ought not to be underestimated. By means of his doctrine of providence, history, more than being vindicated as positive and progressive, begins to function as the arena of divine revelatory activity. The infinite, the finite, and their relation are revealed in the progress of the race. Though he regards Christianity—the philanthropic movement initiated by Jesus for humanity—as "one of the most efficient causes"[40] of progressive change in history, his theory of history and providence awaits the introduction of a crucial christological and incarnational principle. Notwithstanding, the influence of Cousin has resulted in the integration of history into Brownson's thought in a manner previously absent.

Revelation and Scripture

Though no essential change in position occurs, a growing appreciation for the content of Scripture is evident in Brownson's writings during this period. He continues to distinguish sharply between the inspirations of God made immediately to the soul, now expressed primarily in terms of the impersonal, spontaneous reason, and their verbal embodiment and external expression in Scripture. However, this distinction had formerly functioned as a polemical tool opposing an equation of revelation with cold and lifeless forms; it now functions as a means of arguing for the value of Scripture as a natural and historical expression of the inspiration of its authors.

It would seem that Brownson's insistence upon the role of the understanding has been extended to his position regarding Scripture. Though the biblical record is not to be confused with inspiration itself and can only be assented to by the understanding, this assent is granted a value heretofore deemed unimportant. Brownson now recognizes that the inspirations of the impersonal reason require external and natural forms.

Brownson's new found appreciation for Scripture is also evidence of a gradual shift of his opinions toward traditional Christian orthodoxy, a shift that also occurs in his christology. In January of 1840, he writes in a telling paragraph:

> As we grow older, as we inquire more earnestly, and with a broader experience, into religious matters, we have a natural tendency to return to the simple faith of our childhood, and we become less and less inclined to depart from commonly received opinions....As our own experience becomes broad enough and deep enough, to disclose the psychological facts, on which the great doctrine of the church rest for their support, we see that these priests and these fanatical multitudes, that we had looked down upon in the pride of ignorance, have not been altogether in the wrong, as we had supposed them.[41]

Nevertheless, Brownson continues to insist upon the distinction between the revelation of God made to the soul, and its external form and verbal communication in the words of the Bible.

Brownson frequently criticizes what he perceives to be the confusion of revelation with the means by which the proof of the reality of revelation is argued. Revelation tends not only to be confused with its natural means of communication, but also with arguments offered to profer its existence and legitimit its alleged authority: "These great spiritual realities are not dependent for their existence on the theories or the facts assumed to account for their revelation. They constitute the original law of the soul."[42] In particular, Brownson has in mind the argument for a verbal or "plenary" inspiration of Scripture, though the same confusion reigns with respect to the argument that miracles function as proof of the reality and claims of revelation.

Christianity exists independently of all the messengers who have proclaimed it. It consists of the eternal and immutable truths of the divine intelligence communicated immediately to the mind. This is inspiration, a supernatural infusion of light. Though some have argued against the ability to recognize the truths of Christianity as they exist as realities in the spiritual world, this is no reason to confuse them with the means of their natural and historical communication, nor to allow the doctrine of those means to constitute the Christian faith.

The supernatural infusion of light is not owing to any natural or historical means:

> It results not from the natural and spontaneous nor the reflective exercise of our proper faculties, but is the infusion of light from a source foreign to us....Now it is by the inshining of this Divine Intelligence, that we are able to perceive the realities of the spiritual world, that we are capable of religion, of having a rational basis for our religious faith.[43]

Inspiration is the means whereby the divine intelligence is communicated immediately to the human soul. It is literally supernatural, above nature:

"This power we do not hold to be a *natural*, though it is a *universal* power....Supernatural means not only what is *supersensual*, but what is *above nature*; that which surpasses all the proper powers of the being in question."[44] But inspiration does not extend directly to words, arguments, illustrations, or any other natural means of communication of the Christian faith.

The Bible, therefore, is never a sufficient authority in relation to any of its claims. Its authority rests on its truth, not its truth on its authority, and its truth is determined by aid of the inspiration made through the spontaneous activity of the impersonal reason. Though the immense value of the Bible can be recognized through this inspiration, any confusion of the two is as serious an error as the reduction of the reason to the understanding.

Revelation and Jesus

The shift in emphasis from Jesus' teaching to his person continues during this period, as Brownson moves from the idea of Jesus as a symbolic representation and historical example to an incarnate and mediatorial figure. Jesus continues to be less a medium of revelation as a communicator of objective truths or doctrines than a representation of the ideal embodiment of the impersonal reason. However, the importance that Brownson places on Jesus' role as the symbolic representation of an atonement yet to come is gradually de-emphasized in favor of an incarnation that has already occurred and the incarnation begins to emerge as an integrating factor in his thought. Though this movement is by no means completed, the role of Jesus is expanded beyond a mere representation of the union of God and humanity.

Jesus does not merely serve to advance history by virtue of a superior God-given insight. His role as a providential figure also shifts from an emphasis upon his teachings to his person. While the role of Jesus as a providential man receives little specific attention during this period, the importance Brownson attaches to Jesus as incarnate and as mediator anticipates crucial developments in the final years prior to his conversion to Roman Catholicism.

More so than in previous years, the influences accounting for these christological developments in Brownson's thought are difficult to identify. Cousin, no doubt, continues to have a strong effect upon Brownson's differentiation from the Transcendentalists—especially in regard to the role of Jesus. Brownson begins to apply the distinction between the impersonal and the personal reason to the incarnation in reaction to what he perceives to be the limited role that Jesus plays in the thought of the Transcendentalists. But the influence of Brownson's reading of Edwards and other Calvinist divines during the late 1830s also emerges and is evident in a rather sudden toleration of christological and trinitarian formulations previously rejected out of hand.[45] Though not pronounced, this influence represents a step beyond Cousin.

Yet as late as 1838, Brownson still continues to stress that Jesus was first of all a symbolic representation of an atonement yet to come and that the Christian movement consisted not in new doctrines propounded by its founder, but only in the life of disinterested love its members practiced in imitation of him. The originality of Jesus did not, he argued, consist in his nature, for he belonged to no separate order of being; nor in the peculiarity of his teachings, for he revealed nothing radically new. Nor did his originality consist in his practice of disinterested love, for others in history had practiced this; nor in his martyrdom, for others had died for the truth. In what did it consist? Brownson simply offers the standard Unitarian position: "It consisted in the fact that in him the Christ attained to Universality, and that his love was no longer the love of family, caste, tribe, clan, or country, but a love of Humanity; it was no longer mere piety, nor patriotism, nor friendship, but it was *philanthropy*."[46] Jesus' originality consisted of the universal extension of disinterested love.

But Brownson would soon grow dissatisfied with this seemingly superficial portrayal of the role or mission of Jesus and the matter would draw his attention increasingly during the remainder of his years as a Protestant. Emerson again functions as the foil for Brownson's development at this stage. Reacting to the lack of an integral role of Jesus in Emerson's writings, Brownson begins to emphasize the necessity of Jesus as mediator between God and humanity:

> Man is at an infinite distance from God; and he cannot by his own strength approach God, and become one with him. We cannot see God; we cannot know him; no man hath seen the Father at any time, and no man knoweth the Father, save the Son, and he to whom the Son reveals him. We approach God only through a mediator; we see and know only the Word, which is the mediator between God and men. Does Mr. Emerson mean that the record we have of this Word in the Bible, of this Word, which was made flesh, incarnated in the man Jesus, and dwelt among men and disclosed the grace and truth with which it overflowed, is of no use now in the church, nay, that it is a let and a hindrance?[47]

Brownson's traditional and orthodox-sounding indictment of Emerson signals the shift to an emphasis upon the role of Jesus as incarnational and mediatorial. During the remainder of this period Brownson continues to explore and expand his thinking in this regard.

The key to this expansion is the application of Cousin's notion of the impersonal reason, now frequently termed the "objective reason," to the christological doctrine of the Logos:

By the objective reason we may understand the eternal Reason, the immaterial world, the world of necessary Truth which overshadows us, underlies us, and constitutes the ground of our intelligence,—identical with the Logos of the Apostle and the Greek Fathers, the "inner Light" of the Quakers, the Word of God which was in the beginning with God, by which all things were made that were made, which inspired the ancient prophets, was made flesh, incarnated in Jesus, and is adored by the Church as the second person in the Holy Trinity.[48]

Drawn explicitly for the first time in 1839, this application signals the movement away from both Unitarian and Transcendentalist formulations of Christian dogma: "This view would go far to legitimate the belief of the Church in the Divine Sonship of Jesus, and to convince those who arraign the doctrine of the Trinity, that they are as unphilosophical as they are anti-orthodox."[49] Though Brownson's current trinitarian formulations tend toward modalism, it is clear that he is dissatisfied with his previous Unitarian position and is moving to a more traditionally orthodox approach. Likewise, a stronger christology emerges. By 1841, Brownson is prepared to supply some elaboration and explanation of his views as to the person and character of Jesus.

As in the case of Scripture, Jesus' authority consists in the truth of his teachings, not the authority upon which the truth of his teachings resides. But this is incomplete and regards Jesus solely in his humanity, says Brownson. All truth is authoritative and, being possessed by all, belongs exclusively to no particular individual. Jesus' originality and role certainly consists of more than the truth of his teachings.

But the matter is not ended here, for the Church universally regards Jesus as a "two-fold being." According to the orthodox Church, argues Brownson, Jesus was completely human, truly God, the union of the divine and human natures. In this union he was the mediator, redeemer, and saviour of humanity. From these claims emerge two essential points: "1. God was really and truly in union with Humanity in the man Jesus, without, in consequence of the union, ceasing to be God; and 2. That it is God, in his mysterious union with Humanity, that is in fact our Redeemer and Saviour."[50] In the belief of the Church, Jesus always stands for the relation of God to humanity.

With respect to his divinity, Jesus is the Logos of whom the Apostles wrote. The Logos is distinguishable, though not separable from God. His eternal generation can be conceived in the same fashion as a man's reason can be considered in distinction from the man himself: "Viewed in this sense, he may be said to be generated, for the idea of God logically precedes the idea of his Reason or Discourse; but, as the idea of God without Reason, that is to say, the idea of an irrational or unintelligent God, is inadmissible, the idea of the *eternal* generation of the Logos must be asserted."[51] Proceeding from this, Brownson offers a rather modalistic doctrine of the Trinity: "Then we have first, God unbegotten, ungenerated; and second, God begotten, generated, who in mysterious connexion with Humanity is the Mediator. God thus united is not dead, inactive, but efficacious, and his efficacy in this union is God the Holy Spirit, or third person of the Christian Theodicy."[52] To consider the divinity of Jesus is truly to consider God in his eternal generation and in his relation of mediation and redemption with humanity.

Notwithstanding, it must be made clear how it is that Jesus may be regarded as the redeemer of humanity. When the Church asserts this truth, Brownson continues, it is only asserted with respect to Jesus' divinity. The name Jesus is being taken in reference to God, not to humanity. When God is manifest in the flesh, he is manifest strictly and absolutely as God. Jesus in his humanity was not God, nor in his union with God did he lose his humanity. In his humanity, Jesus was in every sense a man. It is heresy, Brownson claims, to take Jesus in his human character as the redeemer of the world. Redemption may only be ascribed to God:

> But is not Jesus, by virtue of his connexion with the Divinity, really and truly the Redeemer and Saviour of the world? Not at all. God, we have determined, by virtue of *his* connexion with Humanity is the Saviour. This is the essential point in the creed of the Church. It is God become man, that is, God manifest in the flesh, that saves; not man become God, or man in union with God.[53]

Consequently, viewed in his humanity, Jesus is not the Saviour, "but simply one of the numerous ministers of God's providence in the education of the race."[54] Confusion sets in when the union of the divine and human natures is attributed only to the man Jesus. Actually, the union between the two natures exists everywhere and everyone can attain the same relation to God that Jesus possessed in his humanity. Therefore, to speak of Jesus' divinity is to speak of the divine Logos that permeates all of creation, uniting itself to all humanity.

Summary: Further Integration

In his attempt to achieve a synthesis of subject and object, and in so doing clarify the conditions necessary for the possibility of divine revelation, Brownson begins to integrate epistemological, cosmological, and christological themes. Though tending toward a platonic emanationism, he articulates Cousin's notion of the impersonal or objective reason in terms of the divine intelligence and cause of creation, and strongly asserts the coincidence of creation and history as governed by the same laws and principles. In turn, he identifies these themes with the Logos expressed as the divinity of Jesus. He has, in effect, brought his adaptation of Cousin into close proximity with an emerging incarnational christology and in so doing begins to unify his own thought.

By inferring his doctrines of creation and providence from an examination of the facts of consciousness, and in turn linking them to a doctrine of the Logos, Brownson starts to extricate himself from an exclusive reliance upon either objectivity or subjectivity, and to introduce an incarnational theme into his thought that begins to harmonize the two without losing their distinction. Moreover, the integration of the doctrine of creation with his previously held doctrine of progress has resulted in the emergence of history, expressed primarily as providence, as an arena of divine revelatory activity.

However, Brownson's inability to account for the historical uniqueness, originality, and humanity of Jesus prevents him from introducing and applying the principle of incarnation in a truly unifying fashion. He is as yet unable to integrate his christology with his theory of history and providence, for history lacks the principle of incarnation. Thus, the role of Jesus is nullified in effect.

Furthermore, the epistemological and cosmological themes adopted from Cousin's examination of the facts of consciousness fail to give themselves over to any theme of creation, history, or incarnation that is more than an expression of mind, albeit divine mind. In addition to his emanationism, Brownson's is not yet free of the subjectivism that plagued his previous phase. As he was soon to realize, he had yet to reclaim the status of the object. It would be through the influence of Leroux that the incarnation itself would emerge as the dominant principle of synthesis, reconciling subject and object while retaining their distinction.

CHAPTER FOUR

The Synthesis Refined (1842–1844)

THE FINAL PERIOD addressed in this study consists of an examination of Brownson's further refinement of the synthesis initiated under the influence of Cousin's eclecticism. The refinement takes place through the adaptation of Leroux's doctrine of "life by communion," which lends itself to Brownson's thought by providing the incarnational principle that his method lacked.[1] The role of Jesus as the objective and mediatorial embodiment of revelation is the key element of the refined synthesis, allowing Brownson to succeed to his own satisfaction in establishing the rational conditions necessary for the possibility of revelation, thus justifying Christian belief.

However, one now searches in vain for a logical argument whereby Brownson infers the reality of the supernatural. Divine revelation as embodied in the mediatorial life of Jesus and communicated through his communion with the race is everywhere asserted and assumed as fact, not as the result of logical necessity. It would seem that Leroux has afforded Brownson more than a doctrine to be incorporated into his thought, but the realization that given the fact of revelation, its intelligibility can be demonstrated by appeal to the common sense of humanity as it is embodied in history and tradition. By asserting the fact of revelation rather than its logical necessity, the Christian tradition becomes intelligible and Brownson can affirm revelation as that which the tradition has always held.[2] Therefore, the attempt to establish the conditions for the possibility of revelation is converted into a demonstration of the intelligibility of its assumed facticity.

The soteriological categories of sin and grace are frequently present in Brownson's thought as he moves toward an affirmation of a more traditional orthodoxy. Two key applications of Leroux's doctrine of life by communion are Brownson's explanations of the transmission of sin and the mediatorial life of Jesus.[3] No longer is the divine principle in humanity the starting point of Christianity; it is, rather, humanity's depravity and need of reconciliation.[4] One simply cannot ignore Brownson's deepening awareness of the reality of sin and the need for the free intervention of grace. Though Brownson nowhere asserts sin as the cause, logical or otherwise, of supernatural revelation, it is recognized as a prevailing condition that requires supernatural revelation and the actuality of redemption. The mediatorial life of Jesus, literally communicated to the sinner through the Church, supplies the means to enable the sinner to repent and enter into the life of Jesus. Brownson's adaptation of Leroux's doctrine of life by communion also allows him to articulate his doctrine of revelation as the dynamic means through which the human race is advanced. The progress of the race is owing to successive assimilations of revelation and natural religion comes to be understood as the amount of revealed religion the race has assimilated during its history, incorporating it into its natural life.

In addition to Leroux's influence, other factors contribute to Brownson's intellectual development during these years. He continues to distinguish himself from the Transcendentalists, especially by way of reaction to Parker's *A Discourse on Matters pertaining to Religion* (1842). Brownson devoted the entire October, 1842, issue of the *Boston Quarterly Review* to a detailed and devastating critique of Parker's alleged naturalism, pantheism, and subjectivism.[5]

He also begins to distance himself from his earlier social radicalism. Though Brownson retains his lifelong passion to establish religion as the catalyst for social progress, he has soured on the political process, especially after the Whigs seized upon his radical "The Laboring Classes," reprinting thousands as evidence of the excesses of the Democratic party and helping William Henry Harrison defeat the Democrat Martin Van Buren in the "Tippecanoe and Tyler too" presidential election of 1840.[6]

Nor should Brownson's continuing study of the history of philosophy and theology be ignored. His thought clearly becomes more sophisticated during this period and as a result he begins to question the foundational presuppositions of his earlier thought. The Platonic doctrine of ideas, emphasized by Leroux, is especially important, as is his reading of Roman Catholic French Traditionalists, which results in his frequent appeals to the common sense of humanity as embodied in the history and tradition of the race.[7]

But Leroux remains the most decisive influence during Brownson's last period as a Protestant. Brownson believes he has discovered in Leroux's thought a method that succeeds in reconciling all conflicting theories, allowing him for the first time not merely to seek after truth, but to proclaim it boldly as he understood it. His regained enthusiasm and confidence echoes throughout his writings of this period:

> I have now, I feel, a doctrine to preach. I can preach now, not merely make discursions of ethics and metaphysics. The Gospel contains now to me not a cold abstract

system of doctrine, a collection of moral apothegms, and striking examples of piety and virtue. It points me to Life itself....I have something besides abstract speculations and dry moral precepts, or mysterious jargon to offer. I have the doctrine of Life, the Word of Life to proclaim.[8]

Henceforth, Brownson would not merely inquire after what ought to be believed, but preach a positive doctrine and faith.

The Influence of Pierre Leroux: Life by Communion

Leroux's doctrine of life by communion, as assimilated by Brownson, is founded upon the premise that the true point of departure for all thought is never found in being, whether of the subject or the object, but in the manifestation of being, the phenomena. The true point of departure is not found in substance, but in cause. This manifestation, phenomenon, or cause, Brownson calls *Life*. To be is not necessarily to live; rather, to live is to manifest.[9]

However, man as subject is not capable of manifesting himself except in communion with that which is not himself, namely, an object. In himself, man is merely latent potentiality; he must be assisted by that which is not himself. It is in the "intershock" of the subject and the object, the me and the not-me, that man lives:

His whole life...is jointly in himself and in that which is not himself, in the *me* and the *not-me*. His life unquestionably consists in the manifestation, or actualization, of his latent capacities. As this manifestation, or actualization, is but the echo of the intershock of the *me* and the *not-me*, or of his communion with that which is not himself, it follows that he can live only so far as he has an object. His life, then, is at once subjective and objective.[10]

The life of the subject results only by way of communion with the object, the not-me. Only God is self-existent being, able to manifest himself by himself alone.[11]

Partaking of the nature of the subject and the nature of the object, the life of each individual is comprised of communion with that which is not itself. Each individual communes with God, nature, and other men as his object. But with God one communes only indirectly, for finitude cannot commune directly with infinity without the mediation of an object. Nor can he commune directly with nature, for the mediation of the body through sensation is required. His only direct and immediate object is other men. Humanity, therefore, lives in solidarity. All belong to the same body, having similar natural powers, capacities, and weaknesses.[12]

It is at this point that Brownson begins an original theological application of Leroux's doctrine of life by communion, applying the soteriological categories of sin and grace to the theme of the solidarity of the race. Throughout history, Brownson argues, Christianity has assumed as its point of departure not a supposed divinity of humanity, but human sinfulness and depravity. Indeed, the "universal conscience of the race" testifies to the fact that all are sinners. Moreover, experience proves that an "undercurrent of depravity" afflicts the human race.[13]

Sinful life, Brownson continues, results from the interaction of subject and object. The preceding generation always supplies the sinful object of the life of the succeeding generation, the subject. If the first man sinned, the sin was necessarily transmitted to the succeeding generation through the objective portion of its life. Likewise, the subjective portion of its life becomes polluted, and its members in turn pass on their corruption to the next generation.[14]

The sinful, then, can only commune with the sinful. The sinful life cannot be transcended except by communion with a foreign power. A supernatural influence is needed to counteract the effects of sin and advance the race. But as finite and natural, man cannot commune directly with the infinite and supernatural; as sinful, he cannot commune with the holy God. A mediator is needed, that is, a "God-man" who intercedes to become the object of the race. It is in the life of Jesus that direct communion with God is found:

> Jesus...is special, distinct, peculiar. Say now that God takes humanity, in the being we term Jesus, into immediate communion with himself, so that he is the direct object by means of which Jesus manifests himself. The result would be *Life*; that life, like all derivative life, at once subjective and objective, must necessarily be, in the strictest sense of the terms, human and divine, the life of God and the life of man, made indissolubly one. For God being the object, would be the objective portion, and man being the subject would be the subjective portion, which united is God-man.[15]

God is the direct object of the life of Jesus. Jesus' life is mediatorial; he becomes the real and literal object of the race, communicating through successive generations the principle of life. The race is granted both progress and reconciliation.

Derived from the doctrine of life by communion, this emphasis on the mediation of Jesus provides Brownson with the incarnational principle required to achieve a greater integration of thought. R.W.B. Lewis recognizes this integration and writes:

> Pondering these fresh discoveries, Brownson put them at last in an order which, for him, made everything clear. The individual needed redemption but could be redeemed only by intense and enduring communion with God; but communion with God was possible for man only by means of the man-God, Christ. Communion with

Christ was possible only by communion with continuing history, or "tradition"—that is, historical Christianity.[16]

Among its decisive effects upon Brownson's thought, the doctrine of life by communion provides an epistemological justification for the appropriation of the revelation of God as embodied in Christ and communicated through history and tradition. In other words, what applies epistemologically to the object, ultimately applies to revelation as fully embodied in Jesus. Finally, one step remains for Brownson: the identification of the institutional embodiment of communion in continuity with history and tradition.

Revelation and Reason

One of the chief implications of Brownson's emerging doctrine of life by communion is his ability to further distinguish his position concerning the origin and ground of religion from that of the American Transcendentalists, Parker in particular, as well as from the French Eclecticism of Constant and Cousin. In effect, the doctrine of life by communion occasions a shift from naturalism to supernaturalism, for Brownson uses it to demonstrate that the origin and ground of religion is not found in a religious sentiment or spontaneous reason natural to humanity. Rather, the notion of a spontaneous reason is replaced by one of supernatural inspiration.

Brownson's essentially apologetic use of the doctrine of life by communion functions as the means by which he articulates his objections to Parker. In his critique, the implications of the doctrine for the epistemological grounds of religion become evident. However, Brownson now limits the role of reason, rejecting altogether an immediate intuition or apperception of God or revealed religion. Rather, the whole subject—reason, will, and activity—receives the objective embodiment of revelation in the mediatorial God-man, Jesus, as the necessary condition for the possibility of knowing God. This section delineates the limiting effect of Brownson's adaptation of Leroux's doctrine upon the role of reason and the resulting epistemological alterations.

According to Brownson, Parker teaches that there is a special or peculiar element or principle of human nature whereby humanity can be said to be religious. This element or principle is understood to be ontological, that is, a constitutive part of human subjectivity, by virtue of which the existence of God may be inferred. But when the religious element is simply posited as an ontological principle of human nature, says Brownson, nothing objective can be inferred.[17] Against the subjectivism and naturalism he detects in Parker's *Discourse*, Brownson argues that to hold to the position that the religious sentiment is an ontological principle of human nature is no sure ground for establishing the existence of God, his revelation to humanity, or the certitude of the Christian faith. If the religious sentiment is a principle of human nature, then it is subjective and has no authority outside the sphere of the subject.[18]

The subject, says Brownson, is the *Me*, which cannot be known by direct and immediate knowledge. The subject cannot be its own immediate object: "Once admit that the *Me* may be its own object, that it can find its own limitations in itself, or that there may be a single phenomenon of life, the slightest imaginable, that is purely subjectivism, and you are in absolute idealism."[19] Rather, the *Me* is known indirectly, mediately, that is, as an element of thought: "Whenever I think, I find myself as one of the elements of thought.... I always find myself in the thought as *That Which Thinks*."[20] But the *Me* finds itself as one of the elements of thought only in relation to that which is *Not-Me*, namely, the object. The self cannot think without the concurrence of the object.[21]

This finding of the self, therefore, occurs not through direct and immediate knowledge, but only in the phenomenon, that is, in the thought through the concurrence of the object. What is established is a fact of consciousness, not an ontological principle. Moreover, this consciousness of the self is always of the subject as subject. One can think oneself only as the subject of an act, as a cause in relation to an effect. In "Synthetic Philosophy," he writes:

> I am conscious of myself only in the phenomenon, and even then only under the relation of its *subject*.... I can define myself only by referring to my acts...my *being* is revealed in my *doing*.... I find myself never as pure essence, but always as cause, and as being only so far forth as cause.... I am conscious, therefore, of myself only under the relation of subject or cause; and, therefore, it is only under this relation of subject or cause, only as projected into the phenomenon, that I can be my own object (61).

The consciousness of the self as subject in the phenomenon establishes no ontological principle, but is simply the result of a higher degree of perception, that is, the result of an apperception. All thoughts are apperceptions, for all thoughts include a view of both the thinking subject and the object thought.

Since the *Me* is only disclosed to the self as cause in the phenomenon, it is disclosed as the subject of an act. But this does not imply that the *Me* is not real substantive being. It is necessary to be in order to act; being must precede doing, ontologically. But the being is only revealed in the doing. Consequently, in the disclosure of the self as an act, the substantive human faculty of the *Activity* may be posited. Furthermore, human nature also possesses the faculty of intelligence. To think is to perceive, as well as to act. "An unintelligent actor would not be a thinking actor. No being but an intelligent being can think. The me, then, since it thinks, must be *Intelligence*." Finally, human nature is also capable of feeling. No one questions the many sentient phenomena that are facts of experience. "I am also capable of feeling…. It would not be difficult to conceive of beings created with the simple…power of acting without thinking or feeling. But such a feeling is not man" (71–2). The me, since it feels, must also be *Sensibility*.

In addition to the three faculties of activity, intelligence, and sensibility are various operations of the mind. These operations are reducible to three: perception, willing, and reasoning. The operations of the mind, however, are not principles or elements of human nature, but merely modes of activity of the subject. Corresponding to the faculty of the sensibility is the operation of perception, the simplest operation of the mind. A perception is only recognizable in an apperception, that is, in the act of noting or distinguishing: "In the apperception we distinguish; in the perceptions we do not. In the former we *think* our existence; in the latter we have only an obscure and confused *sense* of it" (79). At bottom, perception is an act of cognition.

Corresponding to the faculty of the activity is the operation of willing. This operation is the special power of acting and can be distinguished from mere acting in a manner analogous to the distinction between perception and apperception: "It is the Subject exerting its general power to act in a special degree, or under special conditions, with a distinct consciousness of acting, and of the end to which, or in view of which, it acts" (108). It follows that willing entails greater moral import than simple acting.

Corresponding to the faculty of intelligence is the operation of reasoning. This operation is not to be confused with Reason, which is the object of the faculty of intelligence: "Reason, properly defined, is the world of necessary relations, abstract and universal truths, or the world of absolute and necessary *Ideas*, using the word *Idea* in its original Platonic sense" (116). Reasoning consists in the detecting and clarifying of various transcient, particular, and concrete objects through generalization. To generalize, therefore, is to recognize the genera, the real ideas, behind the transcient, particular, and concrete.

Notwithstanding, the faculties of activity, intelligence, and sensibility are not deduced from being or substance, but are learned only as facts of experience, only in the phenomena. Nor does the distinction of faculties imply a division of the essence of the subject. The *Me* is a unity in triplicity:

> There is not one part of it that acts, another part that knows, and still another part
> that feels. It is all and entire in each one of its faculties—a simple substance, with

the threefold power of acting, knowing, and feeling. It must then act in knowing and feeling; know in feeling and acting; feel in acting and knowing (72–3).

The *Me* acts, knows, and feels in the same phenomenon, and in all phenomena. In a personal correspondence with Emerson, Brownson writes:

> I regard man as a being that acts, knows, and feels, and I call his fundamental faculties, activity, intelligence, sensibility. To activity correspond actions, to intelligence…cognitions, to sensibility, sentiment. But as man is…one, and acts always as a unity, of course, every one of his phenomena, regarded subjectively, is at once, and indissolubly, action, cognition, and sentiment, one differing from another only as one or the other of these predominates in the given phenomena.[22]

However, the subject never produces the phenomenon by itself; an object is always required, because the self cannot think without the concurrence of the object. As the self only finds itself in the phenomenon as subject, so the object never appears in the phenomenon as the subject, but only as opposed to the subject. The object is always *Not-Me* (62).

Thought, by definition, contains both subject and object. In every phenomenon, the self finds itself as subject, and that which is not itself as object. The *Me* and the *Not-Me* are found in every thought. Furthermore, the object is not created by the subject, for it is as essential to the production of the phenomenon as the subject. The object is not a product of thought, but precedes thought as one of its necessary conditions:

> Every thought contains an object; and this object, whatever it be, is therefore not me, but exists really out of me, and independent of me. The object I think then really is; and is, not because I think it, but I think it because it is, and could not think it, if it were not. Whatever then I think exists, and independent of me. If I think an external world, then is there an external world; the finite, then is there the finite; the infinite, then is there the infinite; God, then God is (62–3).

If the object is thought, it really is, and is, not as the product of thought, but as one of its necessary conditions. Therefore, in the act of thinking one can be as certain of the object as of the subject. Consequently, the certainty of the object is equal to the greatest degree of certainty that can be acquired, namely, that of one's own existence.

However, Brownson does not intend to imply a type of ontologism by asserting the object as a necessary condition of thought, that is, he does not intend to derive the existence of entities merely on the basis of their being thought. As the objects of thought, God, nature, and other people are not obtained through a process of logical inference, but must be assumed as necessary before logic can begin to demonstrate them. Further certainty that they are not mere products of the thinking self cannot be had except by appeal to the common sense embedded in the history of the race:

> Strange! The human race...all believing what the metaphysicians have hitherto
> been unable to demonstrate, and what the sober-minded among them contend
> cannot be demonstrated! This fact should have induced them to inquire, if, after
> all, they have not erred in assuming any demonstration to be necessary (63–4).

The error of the metaphysicians has been their insistence that the starting
point of philosophy must be found in either the subject or the object. But
there can be no passage from one to the other, no equation between the subject and the object whereby one can be obtained from the other.

The true starting point of philosophy, Brownson repeats, is not found in
being, whether of the subject or the object, but in *Life*—the manifestation of
being. Apperception, or *Thought*, occurs when the subject recognizes itself
and that which is not itself in the phenomenon. Both *Life* and *Thought* are
produced jointly by the subject and the object in their unity:

> Now, as the phenomenon is single and indissoluble, and yet the joint product of
> both subject and object, it follows that both subject and object are, though distinct,
> one and inseparable in the phenomenon or fact of life. Here, in the phenomenal, in
> the fact of *Life*, where only we are able to seize either the subjective world or the
> objective world, the subject and object are given, not as separate, not one to be ob-
> tained from the other, but in an *Indissoluble Synthesis*. This is wherefore I call phi-
> losophy not the science of *Being*, but the science of *Life*; and also wherefore I add to
> it the epithet, *Synthetic* (65–6).

In the phenomena, subject and object, the *Me* and the *Not-Me*, are one and
indissoluble. The certainty of the reality of the object is attained and is posited as strongly as with respect to the thinking subject. Therefore, humanity
believes in God, nature, and other persons on the surest possible basis: "*Because they think them, and cannot think without thinking them.*" No metaphysics
or logic can add anything to this; philosophy, rather than contradicting the
common sense of the race, becomes united with it (66).

Therefore, if the religious sentiment is a principle of human nature, then
it is subjective and has no authority outside the sphere of the subject. Nevertheless, on the basis of this alleged ontological principle, Parker maintains
that the idea of God, the belief in or knowledge of his existence, is given
with the very nature of humanity. The idea of God is said to be an "intuition
of reason," or an innate idea arising from an impersonal or spontaneous reason.[23]

But this may not be allowed, says Brownson. An innate idea in the sense
of belief or knowledge is contradictory, for belief or knowledge is a fact of
human life, not an element of human nature or being:

> The phrase, intuition of reason, when reason is used as Mr. Parker uses it in this
> connexion, reason acting spontaneously, independent of us, according to its own

laws…is inadmissible, though we have ourselves so used it; for the subject of the intuition is not an impersonal reason, but the reasonable or intelligent *Me*.[24]

Moreover, there is no division of the knowing faculty that would allow for an impersonal or spontaneous reason capable of perceiving the infinite directly and immediately. The *Me* is a unity. In the three-fold distinction of faculties, no division of essence is found. In reality, to posit the reason as spontaneous and objective is simply to posit the spontaneity of the *Me* as active and, therefore, subjective and personal.[25]

Nor is an idea ever an intuition of reason, argues Brownson. An idea can only function as an object of an intuition of reason; it is objective, not subjective. Literally, the term "reasoning" should be used to indicate an operation of the mind, the power of intelligencing. "Reason" indicates the object of the power of intelligencing. It implies the world of objective, absolute, and necessary ideas that are the objects of human knowledge, not categories of subjectivity, nor intermediaries between the subject and object.

The objects of human knowledge form two classes, the *Ideal* and the *Actual*. Both are equally real, Brownson contends. The Ideal is the world of Ideas, of Reason—including the abstract, universal, necessary, permanent, immutable, absolute, and infinite. The Actual includes the concrete, particular, contingent, transient, variable, relative, and finite. Though the Actual is insufficient in itself and depends upon the Ideal, it is only in the Actual that the Ideal is revealed and known:

> But, from the fact that man perceives the Ideal, necessary relations, abstract and universal truths, absolute *Ideas*, we must not suppose that he perceives them independent of the Actual, and in an absolute manner. Man is finite, and so are and must be all his perceptions…. He perceives the necessary, but his view of it is contingent; the permanent, but his view of the permanent is transient; the Infinite, but not with an infinite perception; the universal, but always in a relative and particular manner. The Ideal is seen and known, but only in the Actual (124–5).

Consequently, the role of human perception is limited. The transcendental is not immediately intuited. Ideas are objects of knowledge only as they are embodied in the Actual. The transcendental is by no means in the subject, as Parker and the other Transcendentalists contend. This absurdity allows the assertion that the infinite and absolute God is to be found in the subject.

Though humanity is created with the capacity of perceiving the Ideal in the Actual, one is conscience of only a small number of perceptions and forms few thoughts or apperceptions. Each of these thoughts contains a third element in addition to subject and object, namely, the *Form*, or *Notion*. The intershock that results from the meeting of the subject and the object produces the notion that the subject takes of the subject and the object together. "The Subject is always *Me*; the Object always *Not-Me*; the Form is the *Notion*, or what that subject notes, in the act of thinking, of both the subject and object." The form, therefore, is the product of the subject, but only in conjunction with the object:

> The form of the thought, being the notion which the subject takes of both subject and object, is therefore the product of the intelligence of the subject, only of the subject displaying itself in conjunction with the object. The subject taking note of both subject and object, in the fact of life, is called the fact of consciousness. Consciousness is myself perceiving that which is not myself, and recognizing myself as the agent perceiving (68).

However, it is the object that is perceived, not the form. The form is simply what is noted in the perceiving of the subject and the object, that is, the form given the perception by virtue of human intelligence (69).

Under the form of every thought, that is, in every fact of consciousness, is found the subject and the object, the *Me* and the *Not-Me*. The subject and the object, the *Me* and the *Not-me*, surely embrace all of reality; they are essential to the production of any conceivable thought. All of reality is comprised of God, humanity, and nature. Therefore, it may be concluded that God, humanity, and nature undergird every form as its necessary conditions: "God, man and nature, all three conspire to produce each one of our thoughts, and each one of our thoughts reflects them all three" (70). No thought can possibly take place apart from the combined activity of all three.

Nevertheless, though a person is an intelligence, that person is only a finite and limited intelligence, incapable of comprehending the infinity, the Ideal, that lies at the bottom of his thoughts:

> But, if absolute truth enters into every thought as its basis, is essential to its production, yet no more of this truth is expressed by the form of the thought than comes within the scope of the intelligence of the subject. This intelligence, in the case of all beings but One, is and must be limited. Man is an intelligence, or else he could not think; but he is a finite intelligence.... Man, therefore, cannot comprehend the infinity which lies at the bottom of his thoughts. Always then must his *Notions*, or views of that infinity, partake of his own feebleness, and be inadequate, dim, and partial (70).

As finite and limited, reason is always susceptible to inadequacy and error. Hence, the infinite, the Ideal, cannot be established on the basis of a religious sentiment natural to humanity, nor through a reification of subjective activity defined as a spontaneous or impersonal reason. The design of these doctrines, Brownson claims, is simply to exclude all that is supernatural as necessary for the development and perfection of the race. Only through the finite and objective embodiment of revelation in Jesus can the subject partake of the infinite.

Revelation and Nature

Under the influence of Cousin and within the context of a platonic emanationism, Brownson had articulated the notion of an impersonal reason in terms of the divine intelligence and cause of creation, and had asserted the coincidence of nature and history as governed by the same laws and principles. Though Brownson has now replaced the notion of an impersonal reason with one of supernatural inspiration, his attempt to integrate his conceptions of nature and history continues during these years. Each becomes a means through which the race is supernaturally inspired and advanced. Brownson also begins a movement away from the emanationism that had been manifest in his thought up to this time.

The supernatural enlargement and progress of the race occurs through nature and through history. The enlargement and progress through nature occurs by means of the inspiration that results from the continuing realization of the divine ideal in creation. The channel of this inspiration in creation is the necessary and invariable laws of nature and humanity. Following necessarily from the infinity of the creator, the ideal is always enlarging, presenting to the race a constantly new object for its renewal:

> It therefore becomes to the race an *inspiration incessantly renewed*, which renders it in fact a universal and continuous inspiration of mankind; and is therefore sometimes assumed to be *natural*. It is the Logos, or Divine Reason of St. John, which enlighteneth every man that cometh into the world;...It is the Supernatural Inspiration we contended for under the name of spontaneous reason,—that is, the spontaneous activity of Reason as the Logos or Word of God, not man's reason.[26]

All creation, Brownson insists, is infinitely progressive. It grows not by its own inherent power, but by the infinite tendency of its Creator to perfect his works, "to continue the effort to realize his own Ideal."[27] The theme of creation as the progressive realization of the Ideal of the creator as cause is found frequently: "Our only conception of God is of him as cause, creator, but as an infinitely powerful, wise, and good cause. He is essentially cause, and not merely a potential cause, but actually, eternally, and universally a cause. In causing or creating, he is realizing his own infinite ideal in space and time."[28] Nature is not the mere stage upon which humanity displays its freedom and activity, but is itself progressive as God's realization of his own infinite ideal in space and time. It is a mistake to assert that nature is progressive by virtue of its own agency, or through the agency of a religious sentiment or spontaneous reason natural to humanity, whereby progress results through the striving of the sentiment, or reason, to attain its ideal. Both nature and humanity are progressive, but only according to a higher principle.[29]

Humanity is made for progress, Brownson continues. Its growth as a race is analogous to the growth of an individual[30] and occurs through the assimilation of successive truths revealed by God: "The race advances by assimilating to its own life and being the truths which God successively reveals to it, and those which its own generations, by constant striving, successively discern and promulgate. We, of today, are enlarged by all the past accumulations of the race."[31] These accumulations comprise the past, not merely as the abstraction found in doctrines and books, but as living tradition. The higher principle according to which nature and humanity are advanced, through the assimilation of successive truths revealed by God, is supernatural providence communicated through providential men.

God's realization of his own infinite ideal is manifest in nature under the form of ideas. Though transcending material existence, ideas are known only in material existence, without which ideas would be incomprehensible. In every concrete existence, its idea is present as that which makes it what it is and as its possibility of being more than it is.[32] In the form of ideas, the Ideal realizes itself only in the concrete and is known only in the phenomena as cause:

> God is never seen or conceived of in himself. He is to us only in his Doing, only as cause, or creator.... The category of substance is then conceivable only in the category of cause: that is, we know being only as cause, and only so far forth as it is a cause. We seize it only in the phenomenon, the manifestation, not in itself.[33]

In the phenomena, the object is as active in asserting itself as the subject. Thought cannot be produced aside from the activity of the object as it presents itself to the knowing subject. This is simply to assert that there is no passivity in nature. All existences are active as the progressive realization of the divine ideal.[34]

But as the realization of the divine ideal, nature is necessarily imperfect. Parker's doctrines, for example, presuppose the natural ability to attain all the wants of human religiosity and, therefore, the perfection of creation. But God did not, and could not, make nature perfect:

> Now, we deny Mr. Parker's premises. We go so far as to say, that God not only has not made nature perfect, but that he could not have made it perfect. The perfection of God is an insuperably barrier to the perfection of his works. The grand error in all ages has been in assuming perfection in nature, creation, as the point of departure."[35]

Only God is infinite and thus perfect. To assume the perfection of creation would be to assume its full realization of the divine ideal and accordingly deny all progress. Creation, like man, is finite and therefore imperfect. It must necessarily be so:

> But what is creation? We have defined it to be God realizing out of himself his own Ideal. That Ideal, as the Ideal of an infinite Being, must be infinite. Its complete realization would be an infinite creation. But an infinite creation is an impossibility. Infinite is that which is unbounded. But the Creator must always bound, mark, define his own creation, and consequently his creation must be finite.[36]

God's ideal is infinite and consequently the creation is infinitely progressive. This is the basis of the doctrine of progress. But the creation is infinitely progressive only through the medium of the finite. No perfection may be presupposed or, for that matter, hoped for. In an honest and telling paragraph, Brownson writes:

> Man finds rest only in union with God; peace for his soul only in approaching God. He may be eternally drawing nearer to God, but never can become, strictly speaking, one with him. Always then must he sigh for a repose he finds not, and aspire to a good rising far above and stretching far away beyond him. Let no man dream that there is for him here, or hereafter, perfect bliss, any more than there is complete and absolute misery.[37]

Creation is infinitely progressive, but as such it did not begin in perfection, nor shall it end in perfection.

Though Brownson does not completely free himself from the emanationism of his previous period, he becomes aware of the problem through his recognition of it in Leroux's thought. Brownson writes of his mentor:

> Leroux evidently admits creation only by way of emanation, by an efflux, to interpret his own figure, of the infinite into the finite. This determines the character of his theodicy, and proves him a pantheist. The distinction between theism and pantheism is, that the last contends that the actual universe *emanates* from God, while the former contends that God has actually *created* it; and though he sustains it, and is its life and being, yet is he independent of it, and as truly God without it as within it.[38]

Accordingly, Brownson begins a movement away from emanationism toward a more mediatorial approach as represented by the idea of providential men, the greatest of whom is Jesus. The movement is evident in three respects: (1) in Brownson's denial of God as the immanent cause of creation, which he equates with pantheism; (2) in his rejection of Channing's "likeness to God" doctrine; and (3) in the increasing attention he pays to trinitarian doctrine and analogies.

Creation is progressive, says Brownson, by virtue of the infinite tendency of the Creator to perfect his works. But his infinite tendency, and hence its progression, is not the result of a power inherent in creation. The power is a power of God; it is extra-natural, supernatural.[39] To assert otherwise would be to claim God as the immanent power of creation, which is tantamount to pantheism:

> Pantheism consists in absorbing the universe in God; in making the universe, not an image of God, the visible outshadowing of the Invisible, but identical with God; in making the finite and relative forces at work in the universe, not merely after laws originally impressed upon their natures, and which are indistinct copies or transcripts of the law of the divine activity itself, but in making these finite and relative forces identical with the infinite Force; so that, strictly speaking, there is throughout the universe only one and the same Force displaying it.[40]

God is the cause of creation, not its ground, substance or being. This entails "the actual production of substantial being where nothing was before." Failure to make this distinction, Brownson argues, results in positing creation as emanation.[41]

In a similar vein, Brownson rejects Channing's "likeness to God" doctrine, the same doctrine Brownson had valued so highly, attributing to it the rescue from his skepticism of 1829 and 1830. To Channing, he writes:

> I infer that you hold man to be created with a *nature* akin to that of the Divinity. In other words, man is created with a divine nature, and therefore the human and divine must be at bottom identical…. This doctrine, which you have set forth on so many occasions…I must needs believe is the real parent of that deification and worship of the human soul, which has within a few years past manifested itself among our transcendentalists…. Assuming the divinity of human nature as the starting point, as you do, I see not well how a logical mind, not restrained by an abundant stock of good sense, can avoid coming to this conclusion. I must confess that I cannot see how one can avoid it, save at the expense of his consistency.[42]

Though Brownson does not deny the influence of the divine in humanity, he denies that the influence is something original or essential to human nature. It is a contradiction in terms to assert that the human is naturally divine.

The original type of all things, claims Brownson, is found eternally in God as absolute unity and triplicity. This triplicity is of Power, Wisdom, and Love. When creation is considered, the absolute triplicity of God is represented as Being (or the Essential), the Ideal, and the Actual. But it is a representation, not an emanation: "We say *represents*. We do by no means affirm, whatever some may at first sight suppose, that because each being or subject necessarily represents the absolute, therefore each being or subject is absolute, therefore the infinite God; nor a part of God, nor an emanation of God, as pantheism impiously teaches."[43] Each being represents the absolute, but only as subject in the phenomena. Therefore, representation is finite. If one is considered in relation to his phenomena, one may be taken as representing the absolute, but only in a finite and relative fashion.

In each of these three is found a tendency away from emanationism, a tendency evident primarily in Brownson's reluctance to predicate divine being of the creation. In his attempt to avoid pantheism, he is hesitant to identify nature, or any part of it, with the divine being. His movement away from a divinization of nature reflects his growing awareness of the reality of sin as affecting nature intrinsically, as well as his desire to move toward a mediatorial approach, evident in his doctrine of providential men and the role and mission he now assigns to Jesus.

Revelation and History

The higher principle according to which the enlargement and progress of the race occurs is supernatural providence, that is, through supernaturally inspired individuals, or providential men. But in contrast to this argument for the supernatural inspiration that is afforded the race through the realization of the divine ideal in nature, Brownson boldly asserts the supernatural inspiration through providential intervention as an assumption and fact, from which he demonstrates its intelligibility by an appeal to the common sense of humanity as embodied in history and tradition.

The supernatural inspiration through providential men refers both to their own endowment through communion with a supernatural object and their resulting effect upon the race. The means of their endowment can only be miraculous because it transcends the natural: "A miracle is that which transcends the natural, the *generic* power of the being of whom it is predicated. Exalt that being above his kind, as we have shown is the case with every providential man, and you have clothed him with the power to work miracles."[44] Brownson frequently lists ancient Greek philosophers such a Plato and Aristotle, as well as Old Testament figures such as Moses, David, and the prophets, as examples of providential men:

> God, by a miracle, raises them into direct communion with himself, or at least with superhuman excellence. The individual thus exalted into communion with a supernatural object, by virtue of the law of life already explained, receives into his own life, up to a certain point at least, the life and character of that supernatural life, which nevertheless in him, by virtue of his subjectivity, becomes a human life.[45]

The supernaturally endowed providential man becomes the object of communion of those individuals who have direct and immediate access to him. Through him their lives are enlarged and elevated. In turn, these disciples become the object of communion to others, effectively communicating growth to the race. Thus, the supernatural endowment of the providential

man is passed into the natural lives of humanity. Accordingly, the race continually progresses, growing through the inspiration God affords through
specially endowed individuals.

The two means through which God inspires the race are in no sense
contradictory. The divine activity whereby God, from time to time, specially
and providentially endows individuals as the condition and possibility of
human progress, does not negate the incessant realization of the divine ideal
that provides creation with a "law of continuity." In a succinct summary of
this point, as well as his theory of history as a whole, Brownson writes:

> The human race is subjected to a law of continuity, which presides over all its de-
> velopment and growth, whether considered generically or individually. From this
> law human thought does not and cannot escape. The present was elaborated in, and
> evolved from the past. The future must be—so far as human effort is concerned—
> the elaboration and evolution of the present. The law of progress is that of continu-
> ous growth, which is in no case interrupted or disturbed, save as Providence aids it
> on, by granting, as such intervals as seems to it good, supernatural accessions of
> moral and intellectual strength. But these special grants, accessions, revelations,
> which God makes to us from time to time, as the conditions of our progress, do not
> break the law of continuity. They are all made in harmony with one and the same
> Divine Thought, of which human nature, as well as they, is an expression…. From
> the first to the last, the life of humanity is a continuous growth, not strictly speak-
> ing, by development, but by assimilation, accretion.[46]

The "law of continuity" and supernatural providence do not conflict; together they form the means through which the race is advanced.[47]

Life results only through the communion of the subject and the object,
one's natural life only through direct communion with others. They are his
object immediately, and he, theirs. Since one communes directly only with
others, the object whereby he grows must be others. Consequently, for the
subject to be changed and for growth to occur through communion with the
object, the object itself must be changed. But this change can occur only
through the intervention of supernatural providence. The continuing realization of the divine ideal in nature is not sufficient to account for all true
growth and progress:

> Therefore, in order for [the race]…to grow, we must obtain for it foreign aid, a
> power to concur with the power of the race; and to go out of the race, that is, out of
> human nature, is to go out of nature. The whole machinery must stop, unless there
> be a supernatural change or enlargement of the object, or of the subject. The last,
> we conceive, is done, but through the medium of the supernatural change, or
> enlargement, of the object; and it is by this, that human nature itself becomes en-
> larged, that the race rises to a higher and truer life.[48]

The subject grows and lives in communion with a supernaturally enlarged object. As the object of others, the subject communicates to them the same supernatural enlargement. The race is thus advanced.

Brownson posits no logical argument for his claim, yet insists that it is impossible "to explain the life and growth of man without assuming the supernatural, the miraculous intervention of Divine Providence."[49] The supernatural intervention through providential men is assumed and asserted as fact. Given the fact of providential intervention, Brownson concludes his discussion by attempting to demonstrate its intelligibility through an appeal to the common sense of humanity as embodied in history and tradition.

The historicity and universality of religious institutions and beliefs represent more than a proof for the universality of a religious sentiment. This latter, after all, is not natural to human nature, but a universal fact of human life, manifest only in dependence upon a supernatural object communicated through natural means. The historicity and universality of religious institutions and beliefs function as evidence of the supernatural communication itself, for institutions and beliefs arise not out of an innate constituent principle of human nature, but only as the result of communion with a supernaturally endowed object.

> History becomes then a proof of Providence and *a fortiori* of the existence of God. Here is a fact which we commend to our natural theologians. They seek in the order, harmony, and beauty of nature the evidence of design from which they pass by induction to an original designer; without finding fault with them for this...we may tell them that in the course of history, in the passage of man from the savage to the civilized state, in the numerous facts everywhere recorded and everywhere attested, transcending the combined powers of man and nature, they may find evidence much more to their purpose, altogether more striking and more conclusive. The works of providence are a far better demonstration of the existence of God than the works of creation.[50]

The actual growth and enlargement of the race occur through the successive assimilations of revelation. Natural religion is simply that amount of revealed religion the race has assimilated during its history, incorporating it into its natural life, and thus for which it no longer requires supernatural means or authority to be known and lived. "We *are* the past as well as the presentiment of the future. We are the synthesis of what has been, and of what is to come."[51] This synthesis is actual and living; it exists not merely as an abstract, speculative system, but as a historical reality.

Revelation and Scripture

The development of Brownson's doctrine of Scripture during this period consists in the application of the doctrines of life by communion and the inspiration of the race through providential men to the authors of the Bible.

Though he continues to distinguish between the inspiration of the authors and the external form and verbal embodiment of that inspiration, the inspiration itself is now understood as resulting from the communion of the authors with a supernatural object. Likewise, the words of Scripture are identified with the natural and finite means through which the supernatural inspiration becomes naturally embodied in the life of the race. Therefore, Brownson's distinction between the inspiration of the authors and the verbal articulation of that inspiration is similar to that made between revealed and natural religion under the category of history. As the natural and verbal incorporation of revealed religion and supernatural inspiration, Scripture functions mediately.

On the basis of the supernatural inspiration of the authors, Brownson objects to Parker's position as contending for only the natural production and human origin of the Bible, disallowing anything supernatural or divine. According to Parker, those who wrote the Bible were extraordinary not as the result of supernatural enlightenment, but because they wrote with a greater fidelity to their own religious natures than ordinary men.

Furthermore, the appreciation for Scripture that had emerged in Brownson's thought during the previous period continues during these years prior to his conversion to Roman Catholicism. In "Parker's Discourse," Brownson writes:

> We have felt for that sacred Book the greatest possible aversion; we have fairly detested it, and felt that we were derogating from our dignity as a man in quoting a single text from it, without at the same time expressing our strong disapprobation of it. Slowly...have we come from that state of deep dislike to our present state of faith and reverence (483).

The change, Brownson continues, was due to his ability to see in the Bible a significance that previously he had missed. The significance derives from its supernatural inspiration. The Bible, at least in part, is the production of providential men, and is a genuine and accurate recording of their words and acts (481).

The authors of the Bible could not have produced writings transcending their age without a supernatural object with which to commune. Appealing again to the common sense of humanity as embodied in history and tradition, Brownson writes:

> Whence came these individuals with the power to produce such a book; and whence this universal agreement of mankind to adopt the Book as their supreme law? It would require a greater miracle to give to anything human so wide and so deep an influence as the Bible confessedly has, than is needed on the hypothesis of its supernatural origin and production (482).

Aside from this explanation, it would be impossible to account for the lofty position the Bible has held in the estimation of the race.

But the fact of the Bible's supernatural origin and inspiration does not entail its complete infallibility. The inspiration is infallible indeed, but limited. In the first place, it is the authors who were inspired, not the text, which is the recording of their inspirations. The inspiration and authority of the text cannot transcend the inspiration of its authors. Secondly, it ought not to be assumed that further inspirations cannot occur, that new and higher manifestations of the divine life will not be given. The inspiration of Scripture, therefore, is limited (486).

This limitation is understandable given Brownson's distinction between the supernatural inspiration of the authors of Scripture and the natural embodiment of that inspiration in the external writings. Likewise, the limitation is understandable given the limitations of human appropriation of divine inspiration and revelation:

> But it does not follow from the fact of the supernatural origin of the Bible, that its inspiration is full and infallible. The inspiration is unquestionably infallible as far as it goes, but it has its limits. This last fact our Protestant divines are accustomed to overlook. Since the inspiration must needs be infallible, they assume that the *inspired* must also be infallible; and therefore that all their sayings, on whatever topics, must be authoritative (484–5).

The inspiration and authority of the Bible cannot extend beyond that of the providential men who wrote it. Though supernaturally endowed, they were not omniscient, but natural and finite. Their inspirations were necessarily limited, for finite beings can only receive the infinite in finite ways.

As observed above, Brownson's distinction between the inspiration of the authors and the verbal articulation of that inspiration in Scripture is similar to that made between revealed and natural religion under the category of history. Scripture functions as the natural and verbal incorporation of revealed religion and supernatural inspiration. But with respect to the matter of authority, the category of Scripture receives a strong qualifier. Under the category of history, natural religion, as the amount of revealed religion the race has assimilated during its history, no longer requires supernatural means or authority to be known and lived, for private judgment and individual reason are insufficient to interpret it. Scripture, however, requires a higher authority to be known and lived, for private judgment and individual reason are insufficient to interpret it. Anticipating his conversion to Roman Catholicism, this higher authority, under which Brownson would soon subject also history, is the Church (487–91).

Revelation and Jesus

The doctrine of life by communion occasions a key christological shift in Brownson's thought during this period.[52] In addition to completing the movement from an emphasis on Jesus' teachings to his person, Brownson now accounts for the historical uniqueness and originality of Jesus, considered in his humanity. This allows Brownson to introduce an incarnational theme that emerges as the fundamental integrating factor of his thought as a whole. In effect, it is the life of Jesus (not in the sense of his public ministry, but in Brownson's philosophical sense) that becomes the chief medium and source of revelation, the means through which God communicates life and growth to the race. As the greatest of providential men, Jesus becomes the fullness of revelation.

Brownson develops his christology in "The Mediatorial Life of Jesus," a lengthy published letter to Channing. Reflecting his growing concern with sin and grace, he believes himself capable of demonstrating both the depravity of the race in Adam and its redemption through Jesus:

> I think, sir, I am able to show that the doctrine that human nature became depraved through the sin of Adam, and that it is redeemed only through the obedience of Christ; that the doctrine which teaches us that the Mediator is truly and indissolubly God-man, and saves the world by giving literally his life to the world, are the great "central truths" of Christianity, and philosophically demonstrable (143–44).

The doctrines are philosophically demonstrable according to the underlying principle of life by communion.

Given the reality of sin, the intervention of supernatural providence is ultimately needed to explain the progress of the world, as well as to explain the inspiration of the authors of Scripture. Accordingly, Jesus must be regarded as having been sent from God. It is insufficient to claim merely that Jesus is superior to the rest of humanity by virtue of his ideal embodiment of absolute religion; rather, his coming must be regarded as in some manner the expression of the grace of God (149).

The work the Mediator was sent to accomplish presupposes the condition of the race without him. It is at this point that Brownson conclusively rejects Channing's "likeness to God" doctrine as entailing the necessity of asserting a divine element in human nature. The starting point of Christianity is not the supposed divinity of humanity, but humanity's sinfulness:

> Christianity seems to me to assume throughout as its point of departure, man's sinfulness, depravity, alienation from God and heaven. It treats man everywhere as a sinner, as morally diseased, morally dead, and its work is always to restore him to moral life and health; not to a consciousness of the greatness and divinity of his

> soul, but to righteousness, to a spiritual communion and union with God. And after all, is not this view the true one? Is not man a sinner? (151)

Nor is this all, for Christianity assumes not only the actual sins of humanity, but that human nature itself is so corrupted and depraved that humanity is prone to do evil. The depravity of humanity cannot be denied when the universal tradition or common sense of the race is considered, making it difficult for anyone to consider seriously the doctrine of the natural divinity in humanity.[53]

Originally having been created imperfect, continues Brownson, it was seemingly natural, if not inevitable, that human nature become corrupted. This corruption necessarily involved the entire race, for Adam, as the "federal head of humanity," could not have sinned without involving all his posterity (153). The direct and immediate object of man's life is other men. If the first man sinned, the pollution is necessarily transmitted to his posterity by virtue of the fact that he is their object. The preceding generation always forms the object of the life of the succeeding generation. Through both natural and moral generation the race becomes depraved, for sin is transmitted through communion (155–56).

In considering the method by which the Mediator performs his work, Brownson believes he is able to demonstrate the truth of four positions that have been held by the Church generally: (1) Humanity does not commune naturally or directly with God, but only through a Mediator. (2) This Mediator must be literally God and literally man. (3) Jesus accomplishes redemption from sin not only by giving his life *for* humanity, but literally *to* humanity. (4) Humanity is able to live a truly progressive life only if it lives the identical life of Jesus (156–57).

The literal person Jesus *is* Christianity. "To reject him historically is to reject Christianity" (157). It is not enough to assert Jesus as an eminent teacher or perfect exemplar. The wants of fallen humanity cannot be satisfied by natural means, only by real *Life*. Jesus, as Mediator, supplies this *Life* by communing directly with God, a task impossible for finite and fallen humanity:

> I begin by assuming that the finite cannot commune directly with the infinite. Like does not and cannot commune with unlike. Moreover, the finite when regarded as depraved, all will agree, cannot commune, hold fellowship with infinite holiness. Man then could not commune directly with God; both because finite and because sinful. Then he must remain ever alienated from God, or a medium of communion, that is, a Mediator, must be provided (159).

If humanity is unable to commune with God, it is unable to supply the medium of communion. The Mediator must come from God, for the Mediator must be both divine and human or no true communion is possible. He must possess both divine and human life, and possess it not figuratively, symbolically, or mythically, but literally.

The originality and distinction of the life of Jesus becomes evident when one recalls that life is at once subjective and objective, that to live is to manifest in communion with an object. He is literally the Mediator because he lives a supernatural life in immediate communion with the divine. God becomes the direct and immediate object of Jesus' life, which Jesus in his humanity communicates directly to the race. Jesus' distinction from ordinary persons consists of his direct and immediate communion with God. The derived life is literally infused into the race through Jesus' disciples, who in turn become the object with whom others commune. Likewise, life is communicated to succeeding generations, reversing the effect of Adam's sin (160–61).

Consequently, Jesus' divinity consists of a life lived above that of the humanity of his age and is, therefore, historically demonstrable. Predictably, Brownson once again appeals to the common sense of humanity as embodied in history and tradition:

> It is historically demonstrable that the life of Jesus was altogether superior to the age in which he lived. He must then have lived in communion with an object which that age, and therefore nature, could not furnish; that is to say, in communion with an object above the world, above nature, superhuman. Here then is his supernatural character established at once (163–64).

Since the life of Jesus passed directly into the life of humanity, humanity is able to commune with God, continually deriving new life and strength from him. Accordingly, depravity is overcome and progress effected. Through Jesus, human nature has been elevated, its powers and capacities increased:

> If there be any truth in the alleged fact that the Life of Jesus was…a life *above the human life of the age in which he came*; then assuredly has the coming of Jesus redeemed, and communicated to it higher and diviner elements. Human nature is not to-day what it was before the coming of Jesus…. It is false, what we say, that human nature is the same in all ages. The law of human life is the same in all ages; but that life is never the same for two successive generations, or else where were the idea of progress, without which the whole plan of Providence would be inexplicable? To assert that human nature is the same to-day that it was before the coming of Christ, is to "deny the Lord that bought us;" because it either denies that Jesus has come at all, or that he has come to any effect (166–67).

Only by means of the divine life infused into the race through Jesus is growth possible. Confined to its natural life, the race cannot progress.

The harmony of Brownson's christology and epistemology does not give itself over to a traditionally Christian orthodox affirmation of the divine nature of Jesus. It is only the life of Jesus that is considered divine, not the being; only the phenomenal, not the ontological:

> Jesus communes directly, miraculously, with God, and it is by virtue of this communion he lives. This life, that is to say, the life resulting, which is after all what we mean, what all men really mean, by Jesus, must be what the Church has always contended, indissolubly human and Divine. We are obliged then to assert even the Divinity of Christ, in order to state truly what Christianity is. The Church has been nearer right than most of us have supposed. Her error, if error she has had, has not been in asserting the proper Divinity of Christ, but in affirming this Divinity of the ontological Christ, of whom we know nothing directly, instead of the phenomenal Christ, the only Christ to "us".[54]

Brownson's affirmation of the divine nature of the "ontological" Christ awaits his conversion to Roman Catholicism.

Rather, as the communicator of life through communion with a supernatural object, Jesus plays the role of a providential man. He is distinguished from other providential men by his degree of communion with God: "He seems to us to have lived from the moment of his conception…in direct, immediate communion with God, and so had in its fullness, what these [other providential men] had only in a degree."[55] In distinction from the authors of Scripture, who partially communicated the supernatural through natural and limited means, Jesus, to whom the Scriptures testify, communicates it fully. Indeed, since the time of Jesus, no one has surpassed his life. Though many great figures have lived since his time, all that can be admitted is an inspiration mediated through the Holy Spirit, who is the life of Jesus as embodied in the Church.[56]

Conclusion: Revelation and the Church

For Brownson, Jesus not only points the way to Christianity, but literally is Christianity, and as such is "the fullest revelation that has been made to us, and therefore our highest authority for what is absolute religion."[57] Christianity is the infusion of a new life into the life of humanity. However, Channing's reply to Brownson's letter discloses a further difficulty. Channing writes:

> The idea that in Jesus an absolutely divine life is exhibited in connection with human nature, and that from him the blood of atonement flows into the human soul, is the central principle of Christianity. I have long received this idea, although I have never seen it stated philosophically as you have sought to state it…. If you write more about it, I hope you will state your idea of the mode by which the individual soul wins communion with the divine life of Jesus; for some passages of your

letter would lead an incautious reader to think you a thorough-going Universalist and as asserting the actual appropriation of the life of Christ to the whole human race, past and present, will they or nill they.[58]

Brownson had opened himself to the charge of Universalism by leaving the impression that salvation is automatic, resulting simply from contact with the new life infused into the race through the mediation of Jesus.

Brownson accepted Channing's criticism and embarked upon an exploration of the necessity of the Church as the agent of revelation as embodied in the mediatorial life of Jesus. The result is a series of articles that appeared in the 1843 *Christian World*. In these articles Brownson's imminent conversion to Roman Catholicism is clearly anticipated as he responds to Channing's charges.[59] Beginning with the presupposition of the fallenness of all humanity, Brownson argues that the fundamental reason for the coming of Jesus was the salvation of the sinner: "Man, individual, social, and religious needed a foreign aid, needed power from on high, to enable him to break his chains, assert and secure his freedom. The radical conception, then, of the Mission of Jesus, is that of power furnished the sinner to enable him to work out his salvation with fear and trembling."[60] Rejecting any notion of divine propitiation, Brownson argues that Jesus came "solely to the sinner" in order to restore humanity to communion with God.

As demonstrated above, it is through the doctrine of life by communion that Brownson articulates the role and mission of Jesus. It is not through Jesus' death, whereby divine justice is satisfied, not as a teacher of truth and righteousness, nor as a moral exemplar that the aide is afforded. Rather, the sinner can be restored to communion with God only through the mediatorial life of Jesus.[61]

But Channing's criticism has made the problem more acute. Betraying his growing consciousness of the reality of sin, Brownson now emphasizes the necessity of repentance and baptism for salvation:

The repentance which secures the remission, and the baptism which secures the Holy Ghost, are those, strictly speaking, acts of the sinner, which he can perform in a state of isolation from all but the invisible, and therefore outwardly unorganized spirit of Jesus? In other words, are no outward, visible means necessary to be used, not by the sinner, but *for* him, in order to bring him to repentance, and into a state in which he can and does receive the Holy Ghost?[62]

The fullness of revelation received in the mediatorial life of Jesus remains only the "outwardly unorganized spirit of Jesus" unless imparted through an agency that provides visible means whereby the sinner is brought to repentance.

But the sinner does not possess the ability to repent. The Church must supply the means to enable the sinner to repent and thereby enter into the life of Jesus. The Church supplies the visible means and is the "regular appointed medium" of communion with God through Jesus:

> To deny us all outward, visible means or medium of communion with Jesus, is the same thing as to deny that God, through Jesus, has established any regular, certain way of salvation.... We can commune with Jesus only where he is; that is, as we have said, only in time and in space. He cannot be in time and space, unless embodied;...Then either Christ is embodied, lives in a real body here in time and space, which body is our medium of communion with him, or else we have no medium.... Now has Christ such a body, or has he not?[63]

Salvation is possible only through the mediatorial life of Jesus as embodied in the outward and visible Church. The Church, moreover, is no mere "voluntary association of believers for religious purposes," but the real body of Christ through which the sinner is enabled to enter into Jesus' mediatorial life; it is no mere aggregate of its members, but an organism whose members received life through their union with it. Jesus is the life of the Church and the sinner can live in communion with God only by being joined to it.[64]

Resolving Channing's problem with his newly articulated ecclesiology, Brownson would soon follow his own reasoning into the Roman Catholic Church. Not coincidentally, the intelligibility of revelation as demonstrated by appeal to the common sense of humanity embodied in history and tradition becomes the cornerstone of his ecclesiology. Hence, the intelligibility of the fact of revelation is found in the tradition of the Church as the living body of Christ.

With specific reference to his Protestant thought, however, it is the doctrine of life by communion that affords Brownson the means of refining the synthesis of his two earlier extremes by asserting the mediatorial life of Jesus as the fullness of revelation. Through this assertion of the fact of revelation, it is particularly history, or tradition, that demonstrates the intelligibility of revelation, thus justifying Christian belief.

Epilogue

I argue in this study that Brownson's Protestant thought develops through four stages into a synthetic theology of revelation. The synthesis constitutes the means through which the divine and human, or supernatural and natural, are reconciled without losing their distinction. Consequently, Brownson is able to posit a supernatural revelation embodied in the mediatorial life of Jesus, according to which the race is redeemed and society advanced.

In contrast to most of his contemporaries, Brownson is able to recognize the philosophical dimensions of the problem of revelation as it emerges from the Enlightenment. As a result, the problem becomes for him a philosophical inquiry into the relation of object and subject, or more accurately, objective reality and subjective experience. Indeed, Brownson recognizes that the problem concerns the reconciliation of this fundamental duality of modern thought, whether it be expressed in terms of the relation between object and subject, divine and human, infinite and finite, or revelation and reason.

Clearly, the synthesis concerns no mere isolated aspect of his thought, but permeates all his theological and philosophical concerns, and undergirds his passionate belief in the foundational role of religion in achieving social progress. Nevertheless, Brownson's synthetic theology of revelation develops to a great extent in an intellectual vacuum, for during these years no normative systematic theology of revelation exists in America. The question of the relation of the supernatural and natural is in a state of flux during these years. When taken together with a recognition of the turbulence of antebellum American social and religious life, Brownson's lack of a formal education, and his rather erratic personality, this vacuum accounts for the extreme fluctuations of his earliest periods.

Having experienced and articulated positions ranging from an empiricistic objectivism to a pantheistic subjectivism, Brownson gains the ability to recognize the tendencies toward these extremes in the thought of his contemporaries as well as in his own thought. The dualities that Brownson tortuously labors to reconcile in his third and fourth periods are not simply intellectual options presented to him by conflicting schools of thought; they represent the extremes of his own thought during his first and second periods. There is, then, a certain continuity of intellectual development in Brownson's Protestant thought.

Yet, given the lack of a normative systematic theology of revelation in American during these turbulent years, the development of Brownson's synthetic theology of revelation occurs largely in reaction to prevailing American religious and philosophical orientations. His entry into the Universalist ministry and his early appeals to the virtues of enlightened reason are already a reaction to the cultural Calvinism that formed the American religious context. His second period represents a strong reaction to Enlightenment rationality, especially as it tends toward deism, the confusion of revelation with empirical proofs for its reality, and the reduction of faith to intellectual assent to those proofs. Though for these reasons Brownson joins the Transcendentalists in their polemics against such Unitarian rationalists as Andrews Norton, by the time Transcendentalism emerges in the late 1830s as a reactionary force in New England intellectual and religious thought, Brownson has already detected the inherent pantheism, subjectivism, and naturalism of Emerson and Parker, and begins his synthesis by attempting to recover the status of the object. Therefore, the synthetic theology of revelation that develops in his fourth period is as much a reaction to the American context as it is continuous with his own earlier thought.

As one might expect, Brownson does not distinguish himself from the prevailing American schools of thought without being strongly influenced by them, or without adapting modified tenets derived from them. His synthesis is truly eclectic, drawing from the objectivism of the Enlightenment preoccupation with the empirical as represented by the Universalists and Unitarian rationalists, and the intuitional subjectivism of Romanticism as represented by the Transcendentalists. Nor should Scottish Common Sense Realism as the intellectual and cultural bridge between the two be ignored with respect to Brownson's intellectual development. However, the eclecticism and synthetic method themselves are derived from French sources and cannot be claimed as indigenous to America. But as such, Brownson's adaptations may signal that scholars have underestimated the influence of French thinkers upon antebellum American intellectual thought.

Surely Brownson develops his synthetic theology of revelation as an answer to his own religious struggles, as well as the perplexing philosophical and theological problems of his era. Though Brownson recognizes the philosophical dimensions of the problem of revelation, the decisive shift in his thought whereby revelation is assumed as fact rather than logical inference is significant with a view to the religious implications of the problem. Closely related is Brownson's deepening awareness of the reality of sin and the limitation of the role of reason.

Though Brownson certainly does not lose all confidence in reason, the shift to the assertion of revelation as fact limits the role of reason as the means of appropriating revelation. The appropriation is not merely episte-mological, but involves the whole person who receives the objective em-bodiment of revelation in the mediatorial life of Jesus. In turn, the embodiment of revelation in the mediatorial life of Jesus functions as the chief medium of revelation and becomes the incarnational principle that reconciles the supernatural and natural.

As one response to the intellectual problems of the day, Brownson's Protestant thought is important because of this insistence upon the media-tion of the object. The objective embodiment of revelation in the mediato-rial life of Jesus constitutes Brownson's answer to the problem of revelation in the post-Enlightenment milieu. The role of reason is limited to disclosing the objective intelligibility of the *a priori* fact of revelation.

The intelligibility of revelation as embodied in the mediatorial life of Je-sus is demonstrated primarily by appeal to history, though also by appeals to Scripture and nature. The testimony of Scripture, itself a record of providen-tial men, functions as a natural and verbal incorporation of revealed religion and supernatural inspiration. While the supernatural inspiration in nature that Brownson expresses as the infinite realization of the divine ideal re-mains an idea quite distinct from the role of Jesus and awaits the later influ-ence of the Italian ontologism upon his Catholic thought, the idea of natural revelation as the amount of revealed religion the race has assimilated during its history is closely related to the historically continuous communion of the race with Jesus' mediatorial life. Consequently, Scripture and nature are revelatory insofar as they demonstrate the verbal and natural assimila-tion of the embodiment of supernatural revelation in the life of Jesus.

At the close of his career as a Protestant, it is the appeal to history, that is, to the common sense of humanity as embodied in tradition, that exists as the primary means of demonstrating the intelligibility of revelation. Having developed his synthetic theology of revelation, Brownson could appeal to that which he believes Christianity has always taught, namely, the free and gracious intervention of God in Jesus Christ. Brownson's appeal to the Church as the historical continuation of the incarnation and the means whereby the sinner is afforded the ability to live in communion with the life of Jesus, represents the beginning of further refinement of his synthesis. Nevertheless, the complete integration of these themes would occur only after his conversion to Roman Catholicism.

Notes

Introduction

1. Henry F. Brownson, ed. *The Works of Orestes A. Brownson*, 20 vols. (Detroit: Thorndike Nourse, 1882–1887), hereafter cited as *Wks*.

2. Happily, Patrick W. Carey and Marquette University Press have begun to address this problem. To date, three of a projected seven additional volumes of Brownson's previously unpublished works have been produced, as well as a definitive bibliography of primary sources. Each of these volumes contain excellent introductions to Brownson's life and thought during the period treated: Patrick W. Carey, ed. *The Early Works of Orestes A. Brownson. Volume I: The Universalist Years, 1826–29; Volume II: The Free Thought and Unitarian Years, 1830–35; Volume III: The Transcendentalist Years, 1836–1838* (Milwaukee: Marquette University Press, 2000–2002), hereafter cited as *EW*; and Patrick W. Carey, ed. *Orestes A. Brownson. A Bibliography, 1826–1876* (Milwaukee: Marquette University Press, 2001). Brownson wrote seven books, twenty-five pamphlets, over 1500 essays in more than thirty journals, and served as editor of six influential journals, including the long running *Brownson's Quarterly Review*. See Carey's introduction to *A Bibliography*.

3. The autobiographical source most frequently cited is *The Convert; or, Leaves from my Experience* (New York: Dunigan and Brother, 1857); *Wks*, 5:1–125. Also see *Charles Elwood: or, The Infidel Converted* (Boston: Charles C. Little and James Brown, 1840); *Wks*, 5:173–316; and *The Spirit Rapper, an Autobiography* (Boston: Charles C. Little and James Brown, and Co., 1854); *Wks*, 9:1–234.

4. An exception is Gregory S. Butler, *In Search of the American Spirit. The Political Thought of Orestes Brownson.* (Southern Illinois University Press, 1992). Though this stimulating work remains somewhat too dependent upon Brownson's 1857 *The Convert*, some helpful reference is made to Brownson's earliest writings.

5. For example, see Arthur M. Schlesinger, Jr., *Orestes A. Brownson. A Pilgrim's Progress.* (Little, Brown and Company, 1939). This groundbreaking work remains a valuable source.

6. Brownson was born in Stockbridge, Vermont. His father was a Presbyterian, his mother a Universalist. Upon his father's death, his mother sent the six year old to live with elderly Calvinist-Congregationalist relatives with whom he stayed until he was fifteen years old. Brownson probably attended the common schools, but he was largely self-educated and would receive no formal college education. His elderly relatives were rarely able to

attend church services, but at one point as a teenager Brownson underwent what he regarded at the time as a conversion experience at the hands of a Methodist-Arminian revivalist. He did not, however, join a particular church as a result of this experience. In 1818 he was reunited with his mother and siblings and joined the many Vermonters who migrated to what historians of religion would later call the "burned-over" district of upstate New York, so called because of the religious revivals and experimentation that swept the area during the early nineteenth century. The family settled in Balston Spa, where in 1822 Brownson joined a Presbyterian congregation after hearing a Presbyterian revivalist. The affiliation lasted less than a year, when Brownson became a Universalist. By 1825 he had become a Universalist minister and from 1826 to 1829 served three Universalist congregations in upstate New York. Tired of Universalist infighting and despairing of the role of organized religion to effect social change, Brownson, influenced especially by the radical reformer Francis Wright, left the ministry and affiliated with the Workingmen's Party of New York from late 1829 to early 1831. Moving from Auburn to Ithica, he soon began to reaffirm religious principles as the foundation for social change and began to affiliate with the Unitarians. Strongly influenced by William Ellery Channing's writings, Brownson became a Unitarian minister in 1832 and served a Walpole, New Hampshire, congregation until 1834 when he took up a pastorate in Canton, Massachusetts. In 1836 Brownson moved to Chelsea, outside of Boston, and began a ministry to the working class by founding the Society for Christian Union and Progress. It was during these years that Brownson became involved with the Transcendentalists, becoming a founding member of the "Transcendentalist Club," and associated with such luminaries as Ralph Waldo Emerson, Theodore Parker, George Ripley, Margaret Fuller, et. al. By the late 1830s he had drifted from the movement, primarily under the influence of French eclecticism. By 1842 Brownson's movement toward the Roman Catholic Church becomes recognizable and in October, 1844, he converts to Catholicism. Though his thought would continue to evolve, Brownson remained a Catholic until his death in 1876. For biographical information, see Carey's introductions to his three editions of *EW* and *A Bibliography*; Schlesinger, Jr., *Orestes Brownson. A Pilgrim's Progress*; Thomas R. Ryan, *Orestes A. Brownson. A Definitive Biography* (Huntington, Indiana: Our Sunday Visitor, Inc., 1976); and Henry F. Brownson, *The Early Life of Orestes A. Brownson, 1803–1844* (Detroit: Henry F. Brownson, 1898).

7. John Locke, *An Essay Concerning Human Understanding. The Works of John Locke*. 10 vols. (London: Thomas Tegg; W. Sharpe and Son, 1823; repr., Germany: Scientia Verlag Aalen, 1963), Book 4, Chapter 17, paragraph 23; vol. iii, 136.

8. Locke, *Essay*, 4, 18, 2; iii, 138.

9. Ibid., 4, 18, 5; iii, 141–142.

10. Ibid., 4, 16, 14; iii, 112–113.

11. Ibid, 4, 18, 7; iii, 144.

12. Also see Locke, *A Third Letter Concerning Toleration* (1692); vi, 141–546; and *A Discourse on Miracles* (written in 1702 and published in 1706), ix, 256–265.

13. John Locke, *The Reasonableness of Christianity*, ed., I. T. Ramsey. (Stanford University Press, 1958), "Editor's Introduction," 13–14.

14. Locke, *Essay*, 4, 18, 10; iii, 145.

15. Ibid., 4, 19, 4; iii, 149.

16. Ramsey, "Editor's Introduction," 12–17.

17. Thomas Reid, *An Inquiry into the Human Mind on the Principles of Common Sense* (1764) as reproduced in William Hamilton, ed., *Thomas Reid. Philosophical Works*, 2 vols. George Olms Verlagsbuchhandlung, 1967; 1:209.

18. An Essay on Christianity," *Gospel Advocate and Impartial Investigator* 7 (January–May, 1829); *EW*, I, 201–235.

19. See Bernard M. G. Reardon, *Religion in the Age of Romanticism*. (London: Cambridge University Press, 1985), 177ff.

20. See William Hutchison, *The Transcendentalist Ministers*. (New Haven: Yale University Press, 1956), 52–97.

21. See Brownson, "Norton on Evidences of Christianity," *Boston Quarterly Review* 2 (January, 1839), 86–113.

22. Similar to Brownson's successive stages, Cousin was influenced by British empiricism, Scottish realism, and German idealism.

Chapter One

1. See, for example, "A Sermon on the Moral Condition of Mankind," *Gospel Advocate and Impartial Investigator* 6 (September 13, 1828); *EW*, I:161–172.

2. See "An Essay on the Progress of Truth," *Gospel Advocate and Impartial Investigator* 5–6 (November, 1827–March, 1928); *EW*, I:44–75. Also see Butler, *In Search of the American Spirit*, 21–34.

3. Brownson served his apprenticeship for the Universalist ministry under the Rev. Samuel C. Loveland (1787–1858) in Reading, Vermont. His religious studies consisted of exegesis, church history, moral philosophy, and linguistics. However, it is not known what particular works Brownson was required to study under Loveland. See William J. Gilmore, "Orestes Brownson and New England Religious Culture, 1803–1827" (Ph.D. dissertation, University of Virginia, 1971), 323ff. The earliest of Brownson's identified published writings is "The Influence of Religion on Prosperity," *Christian Repository* 7 (August, 1826); *EW*, I:37–43.

4. See Gilmore, "Brownson and New England," 235; David Robinson, *The Unitarians and the Universalists* (Westport, Connecticut: Greenwood Press, 1985), 14–15; Russell E. Miller, *The Larger Hope: The First Century of the Universalist Church in America, 1770–1870* (Boston: Unitarian Universalist Association, 1979), 1–50; and Ernest Cassara, *Univeralism in America* (Boston: Beacon Press, 1971), 9–14.

5. See Robinson, *Unitarians and Universalists*, 47–48.

6. See, for example, Brownson, "Church and State," *Gospel Advocate and Impartial Investigator* 7 (May–September, 1829); *EW*, I:307–332.

7. Other important figures were George de Benneville (1703–1793) and Benjamin Rush (1745–1813). See Robinson, *Unitarians and Universalists*, 246–147, 315–316 for biographical sketches.

8. See Ernest Cassara, *Hosea Ballou: The Challenge to Orthodoxy* (Boston: Universalist Historical Society and Beacon Press, 1961); Robinson, *Unitarians and Universalists*, 61–65, 215–216; and Miller, *Larger Hope*, 98ff.

9. "The Essayest," *Gospel Advocate and Impartial Investigator* 6 (April–September, 1828); *EW*, I:123.

10. "An Essay on Christianity," *Gospel Advocate and Impartial Investigator* 7 (April 4, 1829); *EW*, I:201–235.

11. Daniel Walker Howe, *The Unitarian Conscience. Harvard Moral Philosophy, 1805–1861.* (Cambridge: Harvard University Press, 1970), 83.

12. "An Essay on Divine Goodness," *Gospel Advocate and Impartial Investigator* 7 (February–September, 1829); *EW*, I:262.

13. "The Times," *Gospel Advocate and Impartial Investigator* 7 (April–September, 1829); *EW*, I:285.

14. "A Sermon on the Moral Condition of Mankind," 165.

15. "The Essayest," 97–98.

16. Ibid., 98.

17. Ibid., 99.

18. "A Sermon on the Salvation of All Men," *Gospel Advocate and Impartial Investigator* 6 (August–December, 1828); Carey, ed., *EW*, I:150–160. This sermon was originally published in the *Gospel Preacher* I, xiv (December 1827–December 1828).

19. "An Essay on Divine Goodness," 254.

20. Ibid., 252.

21. Ibid., 253.

22. "A Sermon," *Gospel Advocate and Impartial Investigator* 6 (January 5, 1828), 1–4.

23. "An Essay on Christianity," *EW*, I:201–235.

24. "Mr. Reese's Letter," *Gospel Advocate and Impartial Investigator* 7 (July, 1829); *EW*, I:363–371.

25. "The Mission of Christ," *Gospel Advocate and Impartial Investigator* 7 (September 19, 1829); *EW*, I:378.

26. "Mr. Reese's Letter," 369.

27. O. A. Brownson to Rev. Edward Turner, 17 July 1834; Archives of the Universalist Church, Andover-Harvard Theological Library, Cambridge, MA. Also see "Essay on Reform," *The Philanthropist* 2 (February 14, 1832), 113–115; *EW*, II:122–150. On page 131, Brownson writes: "I look back with startling horror upon that eclipse of the soul, that midnight of reason, from which I am but just recovered. Still my doubts were first awakened by reading Paley's Natural Theology." On page 130, Brownson mentions having read Clark, Tillotson, Locke, and "other giant spirits of other days."

28. In support of this party, Brownson founded and edited the *Genesee Republican and Herald of Reform* in Leroy, New York, for the better part of 1830.

29. See "Free Enquirers," *Gospel Advocate and Impartial Investigator* 7 (March 21, 1829); *EW*, I:276–279; and "Miss Frances Wright," *Gospel Advocate and Impartial Investigator* 7 (August 8, 1829), 252–254.

30. See Edward J. Power, *Religion and the Public Schools in 19th Century America. The Contribution of Orestes A. Brownson* (New York: Paulist Press, 1996), 49–51.

31. See "To the Editors of the Free Enquirers," *The Free Enquirer* 2 (January 2, 1830); *EW*, I:395–397.

32. In Brownson's environment, circa 1830, the term "atheism," as well as "infidelity," connote a type of skepticism and agnosticism allowing for the possibility of the existence of God, the supernatural and revelation, but also allowing for the possibility of their non-

reality. The terms convey allegiance to a probing method of doubt and free inquiry as opposed to avowed unbelief. Moreover, the term "atheist" was sometimes applied to those, like Brownson, who did not accept a knowledge of God's existence, believing instead that one could only have faith in that existence. See, for example, Brownson, "Priest and Infidel," *The Philanthropist* 2 (May 29, 1832), 209–211; EW, II:191–202.

33. "To the Universalists," *Free Enquirer* 2 (November 28, 1829), 38; EW, I:394.
34. O. A. Brownson to Rev. Edward Turner, 17 July 1834.
35. Ibid.
36. "Channing's Discourses," *Christian Register* 12 (January 19, 1833), 10; EW, II:217.
37. "To the Rev. Wm. Wisner," *The Philanthropist* 2 (November, 1831–June, 1832); EW, II:91.
38. Ibid., 96–100.
39. Ibid., 99.

Chapter Two

1. The terminology is that of the Romantic poet Samuel Coleridge and was introduced to the American public in 1829 by James Marsh in his preface to the American edition of Coleridge's *Aids to Reflection*. See Peter Carafiol, *Transcendent Reason. James Marsh and the Forms of Romantic Thought* (Tallahassee: University of Florida Press, 1973), 57–84. There is no evidence that Brownson had read Coleridge by this time.
2. See, for example, "Accountability for Belief," *Boston Observer and Religious Intelligencer* 1 (February 26, 1835): 66–67.
3. See Robinson, *Unitarians and Universalists*, passim.
4. Ibid., 39.
5. Butler, *In Search of the American Spirit*, 28.
6. See Sidney Ahlstrom, "The Romantic Religious Revolution and the Dilemmas of Religious History," *Church History* 48 (June, 1977), 149–170.
7. "Letters to an Unbeliever," *Christian Register* 12 (October–December, 1833); EW, II:280.
8. "Spirituality of Religion," *The Unitarian* 1 (September, 1834); EW, II:358.
9. "Letters to an Unbeliever," 280.
10. "Benjamin Constant on Religion," *Christian Examiner and Gospel Review* 17 (September, 1834); EW, II:362.
11. "Spirituality of Religion," 353–354.
12. See "Faith and Works," *Christian Register* 12 (May–August, 1833); EW, II:230–258.
13. "Letters to an Unbeliever," 270.
14. Ibid., 274.
15. "Faith and Works," 248.
16. See "Principles of Morality," *Christian Examiner and Gospel Review* 17 (January, 1835); EW, II:374–390.
17. "Spirituality of Religion," 360.
18. "Benjamin Constant on Religion," 368.
19. Ibid.
20. Ibid.

21. "Spirituality of Religion," 355–356.

22. Ibid., 359.

23. "Benjamin Constant on Religion," 362.

24. Ibid.

25. Ibid., 366.

26. Brownson is especially owing to the Saint-Simonians for this insight. The Saint-Simonians were the followers of Comte de Saint-Simon (1760–1825), a French philosopher and social reformer. See Brownson, "Memoir of Saint-Simon," *The Unitarian* 1 (January, 1834); *EW*, II:320–329. Also see O.A. Brownson to George Bancroft, (September 24, 1836) in Barnes, "Early Letters," 124, where Brownson writes: "I believe to Saint-Simon belongs the honor of having originated the doctrine that humanity has a life analogous to that of the individual."

27. "Benjamin Constant on Religion," 363.

28. Ibid.

29. Ibid., 365.

30. "Progress of Society," *Christian Examiner and Gospel Review* 18 (July, 1835); *EW*, II:420.

31. "Benjamin Constant on Religion," 367.

32. *New Views of Christianity, Society, and the Church* (Boston: James Munroe and Co., 1836); *Wks*, 4:3; *EW*, III:111. *New Views* is also influenced by Brownson's study of Friedrich Schleiermacher and Charles Follen.

33. The term "reason" is used here in the empiricist sense.

34. Ibid., 24ff. The roots of Brownson's Roman Catholic critiques of Protestantism are found here. Compare, for example, "Protestantism Ends in Transcendentalism," *Brownson's Quarterly Review* 8 (July, 1846): 369–399; *Wks*, 6:133–134.

35. "Spirituality of Religion," 356.

36. Untitled reply to G.B.M., *Boston Reformer* 3 (July 26, 1836).

37. "Spirituality of Religion," 357.

38. Ibid.

39. "Social Evils and Their Remedy," *The Unitarian* 1 (May, 1834), 239; *EW*, II:313. Also see "Salvation by Jesus," *The Unitarian* 1 (July, 1834), 10.

40. "Principles of Morality," 382.

41. "Progress of Society," 430.

42. Ibid, 431.

43. According to Ryan, Brownson hoped for a time that it would be Channing. *Orestes A. Brownson*, 99.

44. "Children's Books," *Boston Reformer* 3 (1836).

45. Octavius Brooks Frothingham, *Transcendentalism in New England* (1876), (Philadelphia: University of Pennsylvania Press, 1972), 198ff.

46. Carey, "Introduction," *EW*, III:15.

47. Ibid., 22–23.

48. "Nature," *Boston Reformer* 3 (September 10, 1836); *EW*, III:76–77.

49. Ibid., 77.

50. Ibid., 77–78.

Chapter Three

1. Minimally, Brownson had read Cousin's *Fragments philosophiques* (1826) and *Cours de philosophie* (1828), which was translated by J.G. Linberg and published in Boston as *Introduction to the History of Philosophy* (Boston: Hilliard, Gray, Little, and Wilkins, 1832). Brownson probably used both the original French and the English translation. See Carey, *EW*, II:16–20.

2. Orestes Augustus Brownson to Victor Cousin (November 15, 1836) as reproduced in Barnes, *Early Letters*, 135.

3. See Butler, *In Search of the American Spirit*, 44–77.

4. "The Laboring Classes," *Boston Quarterly Review* 3 (July, 1840), 358–395. Also see R. A. Herrera, *Orestes Brownson. Sign of Contradition* (Wilmington: ISI Books), 1999, 47–58; and Butler, *In Search of the American Spirit*, 78–83.

5. Clarence L. F. Gohdes, *The Periodicals of American Transcendentalism* (Durham, North Carolina: Duke University Press, 1931), 80. Also see Leonard Gilhooley, *Contradiction and Dilemma. Orestes Brownson and the American Idea* (New York: Fordham University Press, 1972), 33–91.

6. See "Norton on the Evidences of Christianity," *Boston Quarterly Review* 2 (January, 1839), 99–104.

7. "Unitarianism and Trinitarianism," *Boston Quarterly Review* 2 (July, 1839), 381.

8. The club first met on September 19, 1836. Present at this first meeting were Amos B. Alcott, Robert Bartlett, Cyrus Bartol, James F. Clark, Ralph Waldo Emerson, Convers Francis, Margaret Fuller, Frederic Hedge, Theodore Parker, Elizabeth P. Peabody, George Ripley, Charles Stearns Wheeler, and Brownson. Brownson attended four meetings of the club. See Ryan, *Orestes A. Brownson*, 141–142.

9. Ibid., 154–163.

10. See Daniel Walker Howe, *The Unitarian Conscience. Harvard Moral Philosophy, 1805–1861* (Cambridge: Harvard University Press, 1970), 151–173.

11. See "Two Articles from the Princeton Review," *Boston Quarterly Review* 3 (July, 1840), 265–323; and "Norton on the Evidences of Christianity," 86–113.

12. "Palfrey on the Pentateuch," *Boston Quarterly Review* 1 (July, 1838), 299–300.

13. "Two Articles from the Princeton Review," 270.

14. Ibid., 272.

15. Ibid., 274–275.

16. Ibid., 322–323.

17. See "Mr. Emerson's Address," *Boston Quarterly* Review 1 (October, 1838), 500–514; and "Emerson's Essays," *Boston Quarterly Review* 4 (July, 1841), 291–308.

18. "Introductory Statement," *Boston Quarterly Review* 3 (January, 1840), 12.

19. "Cousin's Philosophy," *The Christian Examiner and Gospel Review* 21 (September, 1836), 35.

20. See "Philosophy and Common Sense," *Boston Quarterly Review* 1 (January, 1838), 83–106; *Wks*, 1:1–18.

21. "Cousin's Philosophy," 44. Also see "Eclecticism—Ontology," *Boston Quarterly Review* 2 (April, 1839), 169–187.

22. "Cousin's Philosophy," 43–44.

23. See "Two Articles from the Princeton Review," 288–290.
24. "Development of Humanity," *Boston Quarterly Review* 2 (October, 1839), 454, footnote. Brownson is not the author of this article, but provides extensive commentary in the footnotes.
25. Ibid., 454–455, footnote.
26. "Cousin's Philosophy," 56. On the same page Brownson mentions the influence of N. Malebranche in this regard: "This idea that God really appears in us, that it is by his light that we see, though it may be an approach to the 'vision of God' of Malebranche, is one that we value for its religious as well as its philosophical bearing."
27. "Two Articles from the Princeton Review," *Boston Quarterly Review* 3 (July, 1840), 298–299.
28. "Cousin's Philosophy," 54.
29. Ibid.
30. See "Transcient and Permanent in Christianity," 468, footnote.
31. "Two Articles from the Princeton Review," 301–302.
32. Ibid., 304.
33. Ibid., 310.
34. Ibid., 313.
35. Ibid., 304.
36. "Cousin's Philosophy," 58.
37. Ibid., 60.
38. Ibid., 61.
39. See "Two Articles from the Princeton Review, 317.
40. "Tendency of Modern Civilization," *Boston Quarterly Review* 1 (April, 1838), 221.
41. "Introductory Statement," 3–5.
42. "Transcient and Permanent in Christianity," 453–454.
43. Ibid.
44. Ibid.
45. See especially Brownson's use of Edwards against Norton in "Norton on the Evidences of Christianity," 99–104.
46. "The Character of Jesus and the Christian Movement," *Boston Quarterly Review* 1 (April, 1838), 130–132.
47. "Mr. Emerson's Address," 511–512.
48. "Eclecticism—Ontology," 178–179.
49. Ibid. Also see "Unitarianism and Trinitarianism," passim.
50. "Transcient and Permanent in Christianity," 461–462.
51. Ibid., 463.
52. Ibid., 465.
53. Ibid.
54. Ibid.

Chapter Four

1. See "Leroux on Humanity," *Boston Quarterly Review* 5 (July, 1842), 257–322; *Wks*, 4:100–139. Also see A. Robert Caponigri, "European Influences on the Thought of Orestes A. Brownson," *No Divided Allegiance. Essays in Brownson's Life and Thought*, Leonard Gilhooly, ed. (New York: Fordham University Press, 1980), 100–111.

2. See "The Convert," *Wks*, 5:139–142; and "An A Priori Autobiography," *Brownson's Quarterly Review* 12 (January, 1850), 1–3; *Wks*, 1:214–216.

3. See *The Mediatorial Life of Jesus. A Letter to William Ellery Channing, D.D.* (Boston: Charles C. Little and James Brown, 1842); *Wks*, 4:152–154; and "Leroux on Humanity," 105–107.

4. See "The Mission of Jesus," *Christian World* 1 (January, 1843), passim; and "The Mediatorial Life of Jesus," 169–170.

5. See "Parker's Discourse," *Boston Quarterly Review* 5 (October, 1842), 385–512.

6. See Butler, *In Search of the American Spirit*, 79–83.

7. See "Introduction," *Brownson's Quarterly Review*, continuing series 6 (January, 1844), 8–9.

8. "The Mediatorial Life of Jesus," 169–170. Also see "Introductory Address," *Boston Quarterly Review* 5 (July, 1842), 370.

9. "Synthetic Philosophy," *United States Magazine and Democratic Review* 11–12 (December, 1842–March, 1843); *Wks*, 1:58–129.

10. "Leroux on Humanity," 116.

11. "The Mediatorial Life of Jesus," 154.

12. "Parker's Discourse," 448. Also see "The Mediatorial Life of Jesus," 155.

13. "Leroux on Humanity," 151–153.

14. Ibid., 122. Also see "The Mediatorial Life of Jesus," 155.

15. "The Mediatorial Life of Jesus," 160.

16. Lewis, *The American Adam* (Chicago: University of Chicago Press), 188–189.

17. See "Parker's Discourse," 388ff.

18. Ibid., 395.

19. Ibid., 396. Also see "Synthetic Philosophy," 59.

20. "Synthetic Philosophy," 60.

21. Ibid., 61. Also see "Parker's Discourse," 397–398.

22. O.A. Brownson to Ralph Waldo Emerson, (November 13, 1843) as reproduced in Barnes, "Early Letters," 224–328.

23. See "Parker's Discourse," 395ff.

24. Ibid., 402.

25. See "Charles Elwood Reviewed," *Boston Quarterly Review* 5 (April, 1842), 129–183; *Wks*, 4:316–361; especially 349–352.

26. "Parker's Discourse," 451.

27. Ibid.

28. "The Philosophy of History," *Wks* 4, 413. This article first appeared in the *United States Magazine and Democratic Review* 12 (May–June, 1843) under the title of "Remarks on Universal History."

29. Ibid., 378–383. Also see Robert Emerson Ireland, "The Concept of Providence in the Thought of William Ellery Channing, Ralph Waldo Emerson, Theodore Parker, and Orestes A. Brownson," (Ph.D. dissertation, University of Maine at Orono, 1972), 167–168; Gregory D. Kenny, "An Historical Theological Study of Orestes Brownson's Thought on the Church and the Progress of Civil Society," (Ph.D. dissertation, Catholic University of America, 1966), 76–84; and Gilhooly, *Contradiction and Dilemma*, 94–100.

30. "Leroux on Humanity," 105.

31. "Reform and Conservatism," *Boston Quarterly Review* 5 (January, 1842); *Wks*, 4: 81.

32. See "Parker's Discourse," 406.

33. "Synthetic Philosophy," 65.

34. See "Parker's Discourse," 446ff.

35. Ibid., 440. Also see "Philosophy of History," 413.

36. "Parker's Discourse," 440.

37. Ibid., 442.

38. "Leroux on Humanity," 129.

39. "Parker's Discourse," 436.

40. "The Philosophy of History," 395.

41. "Parker's Discourse," 436.

42. "Mediatorial Life," 150.

43. "The History of Philosophy," 368.

44. "Parker's Discourse," 476.

45. Ibid., 449–450.

46. "Schmucker's Psychology," 29–30.

47. "The Philosophy of History," 399. Also see Caponigri, "Brownson and Emerson: Nature and History," 250–254.

48. "Parker's Discourse," 448.

49. Ibid., 445.

50. Ibid., 420–421.

51. "Reform and Conservatism," 86.

52. The shift is quite sudden. In "Church of the Future," *Boston Quarterly Review* 5 (January, 1842), 57–78, Brownson still extends the incarnation to all humanity immediately. But by the July, 1842 issue, which contains "Leroux on Humanity," the incarnation applies only to Jesus; humanity is regarded only mediately, as adopted in Christ. Also see "Literary Notices," *Boston Quarterly Review* 5 (July, 1842), 383–384.

53. "Mediatorial Life," 152. Also see "The Mission of Jesus," *Christian World* 1 (January , 1843).

54. "Parker's Discourse," 475.

55. Ibid., 450.

56. Ibid., 453.

57. Ibid., 466.

58. William Ellery Channing to Orestes A. Brownson, 10 June 1842; as reproduced in Henry Brownson, *Early Life*, 443–444.

59. See "The Mission of Jesus," "What Shall I Do to be Saved?," "The Church and Its Mission," "Mediation of the Church," "Entering into Life," "The Sacrifice of Our Lord Mediatorial," and "Discipline of the Church," *Christian World* 1 (January–April, 1843). Also see "The Church Question," *Brownson's Quarterly Review* 6 (January, 1844), 57–84; *Wks*, 4:461–483; "No Church, No Reform," *Brownson's Quarterly Review* 6 (April, 1844), 175–194; *Wks*, 4:496–512; "Church Unity and Social Amelioration," *Brownson's Quarterly Review* 6 (July, 1844), 310–327; *Wks*, 4:512–526; and "The Anglican Church Schismatic," *Brownson's Quarterly Review* 6 (October, 1844), 487–514; *Wks*, 4:567–589.

60. "The Mission of Jesus."

61. Ibid.

62. "What Shall I Do to be Saved?"

63. Ibid.

64. "The Church and Its Mission."

Bibliography

Abbreviations—Periodicals

BORI—*Boston Observer and Religious Intelligencer*
BR—*Boston Reformer*
BRQR—*Brownson's Quarterly Review*
BQR—*Boston Quarterly Review*
CEGR—*Christian Examiner and Gospel Review*
CR—*Christian Register*
CREP—*Christian Repository*
CW—*Christian World*
FI—*Free Inquirer*
GAII—*Gospel Advocate and Impartial Investigator*
GP—*Gospel Preacher*
PHIL—*The Philanthropist*
UNIT—*The Unitarian*
USDR—*United States Magazine and Democratic Review*

Abbreviations—Other

EL—Barnes, Daniel R. "An Edition of the Early Letters of Orestes Brownson." Ph.D. diss., University of Kentucky, 1971.

EW—Patrick W. Carey, ed. *The Early Works of Orestes A. Brownson*, 3 vols. Milwaukee: Marquette University Press, 2000–2002.

Wks—Brownson, Henry F., ed. *The Works of Orestes A. Brownson*, 20 vols. Detroit: Thorndike Nourse, 1882–1887.

Brownson, Orestes Augustus

"The Influence of Religion on Prosperity." *CREP* 7 (August, 1826): 49–58.

"A Sermon on the Salvation of All Men." *GP* 1, xiv (December, 1827): 108–16; *GAII* 6 (August 30, 1828): 273–78; *EW* I:150–60.

"A Sermon." *GAII* 6 (January 5, 1828): 1–4.

"The Essayist." *GAII* 6 (April 12, 1828): 117–18, (May 10, 1828): 151–52, (May 24, 1828): 167–68, (June 7, 1828): 181–82, (June 21, 1828): 196–98, (July 5, 1828): 213–15, (July 19, 1828): 230–31, (August 2, 1828): 249–50, (August 9, 1828): 230–31, (August 30, 1828): 278–79, (September 13, 1828): 295–96; *EW* I:97–126.

"A Sermon on the New Birth." *GAII*, 6 (August 16, 1828): 257–62; *EW* I:137–49.

"A Sermon on the Moral Condition of Mankind." *GAII* 6 (September 13, 1826): 289–94; *EW* I:161–72.

"An Essay on the Progress of Truth." *GAII* 5–6 (November 17, 1827): 361–62, (November 24, 1827): 369–71, (December 8, 1827): 385–87, (December 15, 1827): 393–94, (January 19, 1828): 24–26, (February 2, 1828): 46–47, (February 17, 1828): 55–56, (March 1, 1828): 68–69, (March 15, 1828): 87–90; *EW*, I:44–75.

"An Essay on Christianity." *GAII* 7 (January 10, 1829): 7–9, (January 24, 1829): 20–23, (February 7, 1829): 36–38, (February 21, 1829): 54–56, (March 7, 1829): 68–69, (March 21, 1829): 85–87, (April 4, 1829): 102–03, (April 18, 1829): 117–119, (May 2, 1829): 134–35; *EW*, I:201–35.

"An Essay on Divine Goodness." *GAII* 7 (February 7, 1829): 38–39, (March 21, 1829): 87–89, (April 18, 1829): 119–20, (May 2, 1829): 135–36, (September 9, 1829): 294–95; *EW* I:252–67.

"A Sermon on the Word of God." *GAII* 7 (February 14, 1829): 49–54.

"Free Enquirers." *GAII* 7 (March 21, 1829): 89–90; *EW*, I:276–79.

"The Times." *GAII* 7 (April 4, 1829): 103–05, (May 2, 1829): 136–38, (September 5, 1829): 280–81; *EW* I:280–89.

"Church and State." *GAII* 7 (May 2, 1829): 139–40, (July 25, 1829): 240–41, (August 8, 1829): 251–253, (August 22, 1829): 265–66, (September 5, 1829): 284–87, (September 19, 1829): 298–99; *EW*, I:307–32.

"Mr. Reese's Letter." *GAII* 7 (July 25, 1829): 236–40; *EW*, I:363–71.

"Miss Francis Wright." *GAII* 7 (August 8, 1829): 253–54.

"W.I. Reese." *GAII* 7 (August 22, 1829): 264–65.

"The Mission of Christ." *GAII* 7 (September 19, 1829): 295–97; *EW*, I:376–80.

"To the Universalists." *FI* 2 (November 28, 1829): 38; *EW*, I:393–94.

"Letter to Rev. Wm. Wisner." *PHIL* 2 (November 5, 1831): 11–14, (November 19, 1831): 20–24, (December 3, 1831): 37–42, (December 17, 1831): 55–59, (January 31, 1832): 109–11, (February 14, 1832): 115–19, (February 28, 1832): 141–44, (June 12, 1832): 228–36; *EW*, II:85–116.

"Essay on Reform." *PHIL* 2 (December 17, 1831): 51–55, (January 14, 1832): 81–85, (February 14, 1832): 113–15, (February 28, 1832): 129–35, (March 13, 1832): 145–50, (June 12, 1832): 225–28, (June 26, 1832): 241–46; *EW*, II:122–50.

"Unitarians not Deists." *PHIL* 2 (May 15, 1832): 193–95; *EW*, II:188–90.

"Priest and Infidel." *PHIL* 2 (May 29, 1832): 209–21; *EW*, II:191–202.

"Channing's Discourses." *CR* 12 (January 19, 1833): 10; *EW*, II:215–17.

"Faith and Works." *CR* 12 (May 11, 1833): 73, (May 25, 1833): 82, (June 1, 1833): 85–86, (June 15, 1833): 93–94, (June 29, 1833): 101–02, (August 3, 1833): 121–22; *EW*, II:230–53.

"Letters to an Unbeliever." *CR* 12 (October 5, 1833): 158, (October 19, 1833): 165–166, (October 27, 1833): 170, (November 9, 1833): 177–178, (November 16, 1833): 182, (November 23, 1833): 186, (November 30, 1833): 190, December 7, 1833): 194, December 14, 1833): 198; *EW*, II:254–287.

"Christianity and Reform." *UNIT* 1 (January, 1834): 51–58; *EW*, II:288–304.

[O.A. Brownson] to Sarah H. Brownson, (February 19, 1834); *EL*, 112–19.

"Social Evils and their Remedy." *UNIT* 1 (May, 1834): 238–44; *EW*, II:312–19.

"Memoir of Saint-Simon." *UNIT* 1 (June, 1834): 279–89, 350; *EW*, II:320–29.

"Salvation by Jesus." *UNIT* 1 (July, 1834): 10.

[O.A. Brownson] to Rev. Edward Turner, (July 17, 1834). Archives of the Universalist Church, Andover-Harvard Theological Library, Cambridge, MA.

"Spirituality of Religion." *UNIT* 1 (September, 1834): 405–13; *EW*, II: 353–60.

"Benjamin Constant on Religion." *CEGR* 17 (September, 1834): 63–77; *EW*, II:361–73.

"Principles of Morality." *CEGR* 17 (January, 1835): 283–301; *EW*, II, 374–90.

"Accountability for Belief." *BORI* 1 (February 26, 1835): 66–67.

"Progress of Society." *CEGR* 18 (July, 1835): 345–68; *EW*, II:417–38.

New Views of Christianity, Society, and the Church. Boston: James Munroe & Co., 1836; *EW*, III:109–63; *Wks*, 4:1–36.

[Orestes Augustus Brownson] to Victor Cousin, (November 15, 1836); *EL*, 135–45.

Untitled Reply to G.B.M. *BR* 3 (July, 1836).

"Nature." *BR* 3 (September 10, 1836); *EW*, III:76–78.

"Cousin's Philosophy." *CEGR* 21 (September, 1836): 33–64; *EW*, III:79–108.

[O.A. Browson] to George Bancroft, (September 24, 1836); *EL*, 122–34.

"Children's Books." *BR* 3 (1836)—month and day unknown.

"Introductory Remarks." *BQR* 1 (January, 1838): 1–8; *EW*, III:252–57.

"Christ before Abraham." *BQR* 1 (January, 1838): 8–21; *EW*, III:258–68.

"Philosophy and Common Sense." *BQR* 1 (January, 1838): 83–106; *EW*, III:300–17; *Wks*, 1:1–18.

"The Character of Jesus and the Christian Movement." *BQR* 1 (April, 1836): 129–52; *EW*, III: 318–35.

"Tendency of Modern Civilization." *BQR* 1 (April, 1838): 200–38; *EW*, III:336–66.

"Palfrey on the Pentateuch." *BQR* 1 (July, 1838): 261–310.

"Mr. Emerson's Address." *BQR* 1 (October, 1838): 500–14.

"Norton on the Evidences of Christianity." *BQR* 2 (January, 1839): 86–113.

"Eclecticism—Ontology." *BQR* 2 (April, 1839): 169–87.

"Unitarianism and Trinitarianism." *BQR* 2 (July, 1839): 378–85.

"The Development of Humanity." *BQR* 2 (October, 1839): 449–477.

Charles Elwood: or, The Infidel Converted. Boston: Charles C. Little and James Brown, 1840; *Wks*, 4:173–316.

"Introductory Statement," *BQR* 3 (January, 1840): 1–20.

"Two Articles from the Princeton Review, etc." *BQR* 3 (July, 1840): 265–323.

"Emerson's Essays." *BQR* 4 (July, 1841): 291–308.

"Transcient and Permanent in Christianity, etc." *BQR* 4 (October, 1841): 436–474.

"Church of the Future." *BQR* 5 (January, 1842): 1–27; *Wks*, 4:57–78.

"Reform and Conservatism." *BQR* 5 (January, 1842): 60–84; *Wks*, 4:79–99.

"Charles Elwood Reviewed." *BQR* 5 (April, 1842): 129–83; *Wks*, 4:316–61.

"Leroux on Humanity." *BQR* 5 (July, 1842): 257–322; *Wks*, 4:100–39.

"Introductory Address." *BQR* 5 (July, 1842): 366–71.

"Parker's Discourse." *BQR* 5 (October, 1842): 385–512.

"Schmucker's Psychology." *USDR* 11 (October, 1842): 352–73; *Wks*, 1:19–57.

"Synthetic Philosophy." *USDR* 11 (December, 1842): 567–78; 12 (January, 1843): 38–55, (March, 1843): 241–54; *Wks*, 1:58–129.

The Mediatorial Life of Jesus. A Letter to William Ellery Channing. Boston: Charles C. Little and James Brown, 1842; *Wks*, 4:140–172.

"The Mission of Jesus." *CW* 1 (January 7, 14, 21, 1843).

"The Church and Its Mission." *CW* 1 (February 4, 11, 18, 1843).

"Mediation of the Church." *CW* 1 (February 25, 1843).

"Entering into Life." *CW* 1 (April 1, 1843).

"The Sacrifice of Our Lord Mediatorial." *CW* 1 (April 8, 1843).

"Discipline of the Church." *CW* 1 (April 15, 1843).

"Democracy and Liberty." *USDR* 12 (April, 1843): 374–87; *Wks*, 15:258–81.

"Remarks on Universal History." *USDR* 12 (May, 1843): 457–74, (June, 1843): 569–86; *Wks*, ["The Philosophy of History"], 4:361–423.

[O.A. Brownson] to Ralph Waldo Emerson, (November 13, 1843); *EL*, 324–28.

"Introduction." *BRQR* (whole volume series) 6 (January, 1844): 1–28.

"No Church, No Reform." *BRQR* 6 (April, 1844): 175–94; *Wks*, 4:496–512.

"Church Unity and Social Amelioration." *BRQR* 6 (July, 1844): 310–327; *Wks*, 4:512–26.

"The Anglican Church Schismatic." *BRQR* 6 (October, 1844): 487–514; *Wks*, 4:567–89.

"Protestantism ends in Transcendentalism." *BRQR* 8 (July, 1846): 369–99; *Wks*, 6:113–134.

"An a priori Autobiography." *BRQR* 12 (January, 1850): 1–38; *Wks*, 1:214–252.

The Convert; or, Leaves from my Experience. New York: Dunigan and Brother, 1857; *Wks*, 5:1–200.

Index